Python Programming For Beginners

A Comprehensive Guide To Learning Python Syntax, Data Types, Control Structures, Functions And Modules

Brenson E. Lee

Table Of Content

DISCLAIMER

The authors and publishers of "Python Programming For Beginners" have diligently striven to ensure the accuracy and completeness of the information contained within this book at the time of publication. However, it is crucial to acknowledge that the field of software development, including Python Programming, is characterized by rapid advancements and evolving best practices.

Therefore, the authors and publishers offer no warranty, express or implied, regarding the enduring accuracy, completeness, suitability, or effectiveness of the information presented herein. Readers are strongly encouraged to remain abreast of the latest developments in Python Programming, associated technologies, and industry best practices through continued learning and engagement with relevant resources.

The authors and publishers shall not be held liable for any errors, omissions, or any losses or damages of any kind arising from the use of, or reliance upon, the information contained within this book. This includes, but is not limited to, incidental, consequential, or punitive damages.

INTRODUCTION

Have you ever wished you could automate tedious tasks, analyze data with ease, or even build your own websites and applications? If so, you've come to the right place. This book is your gateway to unlocking the power of Python, one of the most versatile and in-demand programming languages in the world today.

Whether you're a complete beginner with no coding experience or someone looking to add Python to your skillset, this book will guide you through the fundamentals and beyond. We'll embark on a journey together, starting with the very basics of Python syntax and data types, and gradually progressing to more advanced concepts like control flow, functions, and data structures.

What makes this book different?

- **Clarity and Simplicity:** We've meticulously crafted this book with a focus on clear, concise explanations and jargon-free language. Even the most complex concepts are broken down into digestible steps, ensuring that you grasp the fundamentals with ease.

- **Hands-on Learning:** We believe that the best way to learn is by doing. Throughout this book, you'll find numerous interactive exercises, coding challenges, and mini-projects that will solidify your understanding and build your confidence.
- **Real-World Relevance:** We've carefully chosen examples and projects that resonate with real-world applications, making your learning experience both engaging and practical.
- **Modern and Up-to-Date:** This book is based on the latest version of Python, ensuring you're learning the most current and relevant techniques.

By the end of this book, you'll be able to:

- **Write clean and efficient Python code.**
- **Understand fundamental programming concepts like variables, data types, and control flow.**
- **Work with data structures like lists, tuples, and dictionaries.**
- **Define and use functions to organize your code.**
- **Handle errors and debug your programs.**
- **And much more!**

Who is this book for?

This book is perfect for:

- Absolute beginners with no prior programming experience.
- Students learning Python in school or college.
- Professionals from any field who want to add Python to their skillset.
- Anyone curious about programming and eager to explore the possibilities of Python.

No matter your background or experience, this book will equip you with the knowledge and skills you need to embark on your Python programming journey. So, let's dive in and discover the exciting world of Python together!

Part 1: Foundations of Python

Chapter 1: Welcome to the World of Python

Why Python?

In the vast and ever-evolving landscape of programming languages, Python has emerged as a shining star, captivating both seasoned developers and eager beginners alike. But what is it about Python that has propelled it to such heights of popularity? In this section, we'll delve into the key reasons why Python has become the language of choice for countless individuals and organizations worldwide.

1.1.1 Simplicity: Readability and Ease of Learning

Python's greatest strength lies in its remarkable simplicity. Designed with a focus on readability, Python's syntax closely resembles plain English, making it incredibly intuitive and easy to learn. This emphasis on clarity reduces the cognitive burden on programmers, allowing them to express complex ideas with fewer lines of code.

Imagine you want to display the text "Hello, world!" on your screen. In many programming languages, this would involve multiple lines of code and intricate syntax. In Python, it's as simple as:

Python

```
print("Hello, world!")
```

This straightforwardness makes Python an ideal choice for beginners, enabling them to grasp fundamental programming concepts quickly and embark on their coding journey with confidence.

1.1.2 Versatility: A Multi-Purpose Powerhouse

Python's versatility is another key factor contributing to its widespread adoption. It's a truly general-purpose language, capable of tackling a wide range of tasks across diverse domains. Whether you're interested in:

- **Web Development:** Building dynamic websites and web applications with frameworks like Django and Flask.
- **Data Science and Machine Learning:** Analyzing data, creating visualizations, and developing intelligent algorithms with

libraries like Pandas, NumPy, and Scikit-learn.

- **Scripting and Automation:** Automating repetitive tasks, managing system administration, and extracting information from websites.
- **Desktop Applications:** Creating cross-platform applications with graphical user interfaces.
- **Game Development:** Developing interactive games with libraries like Pygame.

Python has the tools and libraries to support your endeavors. This adaptability makes Python a valuable asset for any programmer, as it can be used across different facets of a project, eliminating the need to switch between languages.

1.1.3 Community: A Thriving Ecosystem of Support

Behind every successful programming language is a vibrant and supportive community, and Python is no exception. The Python community is renowned for its inclusivity, helpfulness, and collaborative spirit. This translates into:

- **Extensive Documentation:** A wealth of well-maintained documentation, tutorials, and online resources are readily available to guide you through any challenges you encounter.

- **Active Forums and Communities:** Online forums and communities provide platforms to ask questions, seek advice, and connect with fellow Python enthusiasts.
- **Open-Source Libraries and Frameworks:** A vast ecosystem of open-source libraries and frameworks constantly expands Python's capabilities, providing ready-made solutions for various tasks.

This strong community support ensures that Python remains up-to-date with the latest trends and technologies, making it a future-proof choice for your programming journey.

In essence, Python's winning combination of simplicity, versatility, and community support has cemented its position as a leading programming language in today's tech-driven world. Whether you're a novice taking your first steps into the world of code or an experienced developer seeking a powerful and adaptable tool, Python offers an unparalleled platform for turning your ideas into reality.

Setting Up Your Python Environment (Installation, IDEs)

Now that you're acquainted with the compelling reasons to learn Python, let's get your computer ready for coding! This section will guide you through the essential steps of setting up your Python environment, ensuring you have the necessary tools to write and execute Python code.

1.2.1 Installing Python

The first step is to install Python on your system. Don't worry, it's a straightforward process! Here's how:

1. **Download the Installer:** Head over to the official Python website (python.org) and navigate to the "Downloads" section. Choose the latest stable version of Python (Python 3.11 or later is recommended) that's compatible with your operating system (Windows, macOS, or Linux).
2. **Run the Installer:** Once the installer is downloaded, double-click it to run it. Follow the on-screen instructions, making sure to check the box that says "Add Python to PATH" (this makes it easier to run Python from your command line or terminal).

3. **Verify the Installation:** To confirm that Python has been successfully installed, open your command line or terminal and type `python --version` or `python3 --version`. You should see the installed Python version displayed.

1.2.2 Choosing an IDE (Integrated Development Environment)

While you can write Python code in a simple text editor, using an IDE can significantly enhance your coding experience. IDEs provide a range of helpful features, such as:

- **Code highlighting:** Makes your code easier to read and understand.
- **Autocompletion:** Suggests code completions as you type, saving time and reducing errors.
- **Debugging tools:** Help you identify and fix errors in your code.
- **Integrated terminal:** Allows you to run your code directly within the IDE.

Here are some popular IDEs for Python:

- **VS Code (Visual Studio Code):** A lightweight and highly customizable IDE with excellent Python support.
- **PyCharm:** A powerful IDE specifically designed for Python development.
- **Thonny:** A beginner-friendly IDE with a simple interface and built-in debugger.
- **Sublime Text:** A versatile text editor with excellent Python support through plugins.

The choice of IDE depends on your personal preferences and needs. Feel free to experiment with different IDEs to find the one that suits you best.

1.2.3 Using a Text Editor and the Command Line

If you prefer a minimalist approach, you can also write Python code in a basic text editor (like Notepad on Windows or TextEdit on macOS) and run it from your command line or terminal. Here's how:

1. **Write your code:** Create a new file in your text editor and write your Python code. Save the file with a `.py` extension (e.g., `my_program.py`).

2. **Open your command line/terminal:** Navigate to the directory where you saved your file using the `cd` command.
3. **Run your code:** Type `python my_program.py` (or `python3 my_program.py`) and press Enter. Your Python code will be executed, and the output will be displayed in the terminal.

By following these steps, you'll have a fully functional Python environment ready to go. Now you're all set to dive into the exciting world of Python programming!

Writing Your First Python Program ("Hello, World!", Basic Syntax)

It's time to dive into the heart of Python and write your very first program! We'll start with the quintessential "Hello, world!" program, a time-honored tradition in the world of programming. This simple exercise will introduce you to Python's basic syntax and give you a taste of how code is written and executed.

1.3.1 The "Hello, World!" Program

Open your chosen IDE or text editor and type the following line of code:

Python

```
print("Hello, world!")
```

That's it! This single line of code is all it takes to display the message "Hello, world!" on your screen. Let's break down what's happening:

- `print()`: This is a built-in function in Python that displays output to the console.
- `"Hello, world!"`: This is a string literal, which is a sequence of characters enclosed in quotation marks. It represents the text you want to display.

1.3.2 Running Your Code

Now, let's run this code and witness the magic of Python in action.

- **If you're using an IDE:** Most IDEs have a "Run" button or a menu option to execute your code. Click it, and you should see "Hello, world!" appear in the IDE's console or output window.
- **If you're using a text editor and the command line:**

1. Save your code as a Python file (e.g., `hello.py`).
2. Open your command line or terminal and navigate to the directory where you saved the file.
3. Type `python hello.py` (or `python3 hello.py`) and press Enter.

You should see the output "Hello, world!" printed in your terminal. Congratulations! You've just written and executed your first Python program.

1.3.3 Basic Syntax Rules

While this program is simple, it demonstrates some fundamental syntax rules in Python:

- **Case-sensitivity:** Python is case-sensitive, so `print()` is not the same as `Print()`.
- **Indentation:** Indentation (using spaces or tabs) is crucial in Python. It defines blocks of code, which we'll explore later. For now, ensure your code is aligned to the left margin.
- **Parentheses:** Functions in Python use parentheses to enclose their arguments (the values they operate on). In this case, `"Hello, world!"` is the argument passed to the `print()` function.

1.3.4 Beyond "Hello, World!"

You can use the `print()` function to display other types of data as well. For example:

Python

```
print(5)              # Prints the integer 5
print(3.14)                    #    Prints    the
floating-point number 3.14
print(True)               #  Prints  the  boolean
value True
```

You can even combine different data types within a single `print()` statement:

Python

```
print("The  answer  is",  42)    # Output:  The
answer is 42
```

As you progress through this book, you'll learn how to use Python to perform more complex operations and build exciting projects.

Chapter 2: Data Types and Variables

Understanding Data Types (Integers, Floats, Strings, Booleans)

Just like the physical world is made up of different materials like wood, metal, and plastic, the world of programming relies on various types of data. To work effectively with this data, we need a way to classify it. This is where the concept of "data types" comes in.

Think of data types as labels that we attach to information. These labels help Python understand how to handle and process the data. Python is smart – it can often figure out the data type on its own (this is called "dynamic typing"). However, it's essential for you, the programmer, to be aware of these types to write code that behaves as expected.

Let's explore some of the fundamental data types that form the foundation of Python programming:

2.1.1 Integers: The Counting Numbers

When you need to work with whole numbers, whether it's counting objects, tracking scores in a game, or representing years, you'll use integers.

These are your everyday numbers, both positive and negative, without any decimal components.

Examples:

Python

```
player_score = 100
current_year = 2024
items_in_cart = 5
```

2.1.2   Floating-Point   Numbers: Handling Decimals

For situations that demand precision, such as scientific calculations, financial transactions, or measuring temperatures, we turn to floating-point numbers. These numbers include a decimal point, allowing us to represent values with fractional parts.

Examples:

Python

```
product_price = 19.99
room_temperature = 22.5
earth_gravity = 9.81
```

2.1.3 Strings: Representing Text

Text is everywhere in programming, from displaying messages to users to storing names, addresses, and even entire articles. In Python, we use strings to work with this textual data. Strings are sequences of characters enclosed within single (') or double (") quotes.

Examples:

Python

```
user_name = "Bob"
welcome_message = 'Welcome to our website!'
product_description    =    "This    is    a
high-quality product."
```

2.1.4 Booleans: True or False

Booleans are the simplest data type, representing only two possible values: True or False. They are essential for making decisions in your code and controlling how your programs behave.

Examples:

Python

```
is_logged_in = True
is_item_available = False
is_valid_password = len(password) >= 8 #
Checks if the password has at least 8
characters
```

2.1.5 Changing Data Types: Type Conversion

Sometimes, you'll need to transform data from one type to another. Python provides handy tools for this:

- `int()`: Turns a value into an integer.
- `float()`: Turns a value into a floating-point number.
- `str()`: Turns a value into a string.
- `bool()`: Turns a value into a boolean.

Examples:

Python

```python
product_price = "24.95"
price_as_number = float(product_price) #
Converts the string "24.95" to the number
24.95

user_age = 30
age_as_text = str(user_age) # Converts the
number 30 to the string "30"
```

Mastering data types is crucial for writing effective Python code. By understanding how data is categorized and handled, you can create programs that accurately process information and produce the desired results. Next, we'll explore how to store and work with data using variables.

Working with Variables (Naming, Assignment, Operations)

Imagine variables as containers that hold your data in a program. They give your data a name and a place to reside in the computer's memory, allowing you to access and manipulate it throughout your code. Think of them as labeled boxes where you can store different types of items (your data).

2.2.1 Naming Variables: Choosing Meaningful Labels

Choosing appropriate names for your variables is crucial for writing readable and maintainable code. Here are some guidelines:

- **Descriptive Names:** Use names that clearly indicate the purpose of the variable. For example, `user_age` is more informative than just `age`.
- **Snake Case:** In Python, it's common to use lowercase words separated by underscores (_) for variable names (e.g., `total_amount`, `first_name`).
- **Avoid Reserved Words:** Don't use Python's reserved words (like `if`, `else`, `for`, `while`, `print`, etc.) as variable names.

Examples of valid variable names:

Python

```python
user_name = "Alice"
item_price = 19.99
is_valid = True
```

2.2.2 Assigning Values: Filling the Container

The assignment operator (=) is used to assign a value to a variable. The value on the right side of the = is stored in the variable on the left side.

Examples:

Python

```
age = 30            # Assigns the integer 30
to the variable 'age'
name = "Bob"        # Assigns the string
"Bob" to the variable 'name'
pi = 3.14159        # Assigns the float
3.14159 to the variable 'pi'
```

2.2.3 Operations with Variables: Manipulating Data

Once you have data stored in variables, you can use them in various operations:

- **Arithmetic Operations:** Perform calculations with numerical variables.

Python

```
price = 10
quantity = 5
total_cost = price * quantity  # total_cost
will be 50
```

- **String Concatenation:** Combine strings using the + operator.

Python

```
first_name = "John"
last_name = "Doe"
full_name = first_name + " " + last_name  #
full_name will be "John Doe"[1]
```

- **Comparison Operations:** Compare values using operators like == (equals), != (not equals), > (greater than), < (less than), etc.

Python

```
age = 25
is_adult = age >= 18  # is_adult will be
True
```

- **Updating Variables:** Modify the value of a variable by assigning a new value to it.

Python

```
count = 10
count = count + 1   # count will now be 11
```

By understanding how to name, assign values to, and perform operations with variables, you gain the ability to store, manipulate, and process data effectively in your Python programs. These fundamental concepts lay the groundwork for building more complex and dynamic applications.

Input and Output (Getting User Input, Printing Results)

Up until now, our programs have been a bit one-sided. They've been displaying information, but not really listening to us. To create truly interactive programs, we need ways to get input from the user and display results back to them. That's where input and output come in.

2.3.1 Getting User Input: The `input()` Function

The `input()` function allows your program to pause and wait for the user to type something using the keyboard. Whatever the user types is then captured by your program as a string.

Python

```python
name = input("Please enter your name: ")
print("Hello, " + name + "!")
```

In this example, the program first displays the message "Please enter your name: ". The `input()` function then waits for the user to type their name and press Enter. The entered name is stored in the `name` variable. Finally, the program greets the user using their name.

2.3.2 Printing Results: The `print()` Function

You've already met the `print()` function, our primary tool for displaying output to the console. It takes one or more values as arguments and displays them on the screen.

Python

```
age = 25
print("You are", age, "years old.")
```

This code snippet prints the following output:

```
You are 25 years old.
```

2.3.3 Combining Input and Output

Let's combine `input()` and `print()` to create a simple interactive program that calculates the area of a rectangle:

Python

```
length = float(input("Enter the length of
the rectangle: "))
width = float(input("Enter the width of the
rectangle: "))
area = length * width
print("The area of the rectangle is", area)
```

In this program:

1. We use `input()` to get the length and width from the user.
2. We use `float()` to convert the user's input (which is initially a string) into floating-point numbers, allowing us to perform calculations.
3. We calculate the area by multiplying `length` and `width`.
4. We use `print()` to display the result to the user.

2.3.4 Formatting Output

You can make your output more readable and presentable by using f-strings (formatted string literals). F-strings allow you to embed variables and expressions directly within a string by placing them in curly braces `{}`.

Python

```python
name = "Alice"
age = 30
print(f"Hello, {name}! You are {age} years old.")
```

This will produce the same output as before:

```
Hello, Alice! You are 30 years old.
```

F-strings provide a concise and powerful way to format your output, making your programs more user-friendly.

By mastering input and output, you can create dynamic programs that respond to user actions and provide meaningful feedback. This opens up a world of possibilities for building interactive applications and tools.

Chapter 3: Operators and Expressions

Arithmetic Operators (+, -, *, /, //, %, **)

Just like in everyday math, Python provides a set of arithmetic operators that allow you to perform calculations on numerical data. These operators are the building blocks for creating expressions that evaluate to numerical results. Let's dive into the essential arithmetic operators in Python:

3.1.1 Addition (+)

The addition operator adds two values together.

Python

```
result = 5 + 3   # result will be 8
```

3.1.2 Subtraction (-)

The subtraction operator subtracts one value from another.

Python

```
result = 10 - 4   # result will be 6
```

3.1.3 Multiplication (*)

The multiplication operator multiplies two values.

Python

```
result = 7 * 2   # result will be 14
```

3.1.4 Division (/)

The division operator divides one value by another, producing a floating-point result.

Python

```
result = 15 / 4   # result will be 3.75
```

3.1.5 Floor Division (//)

The floor division operator divides one value by another and rounds the result down to the nearest integer.

Python

```
result = 15 // 4  # result will be 3
```

3.1.6 Modulo (%)

The modulo operator returns the remainder of a division operation.

Python

```
result = 15 % 4  # result will be 3
```

3.1.7 Exponentiation (**)

The exponentiation operator raises a value to a given power.

Python

```
result = 2 ** 3   # result will be 8 (2 * 2
* 2)
```

3.1.8 Operator Precedence

Just like in regular math, Python follows a specific order of operations when evaluating expressions with multiple operators. The order of precedence is as follows:

1. **Parentheses:** ()
2. **Exponentiation:** **
3. **Multiplication, Division, Floor Division, Modulo:** *, /, //, % (from left to right)
4. **Addition and Subtraction:** +, - (from left to right)

You can use parentheses to override the default precedence and force certain operations to be evaluated first.

Python

```
result = 5 + 3 * 2   # result will be 11
(multiplication first)
result = (5 + 3) * 2   # result will be 16
(addition first)
```

3.1.9 Combining Operators with Variables

You can use arithmetic operators with variables to perform calculations on data stored in your program.

Python

```
price = 10.5
quantity = 3
total_cost = price * quantity  # total_cost
will be 31.5

discount = 0.1
discounted_price = price * (1 - discount)
# discounted_price will be 9.45
```

By understanding arithmetic operators and their precedence, you can create complex expressions to perform a wide range of calculations in your Python programs. These operators are fundamental building blocks for manipulating numerical data and creating dynamic applications.

Comparison Operators (==, !=, >, <, >=, <=)

Comparison operators allow you to compare two values and determine their relationship. They are essential for making decisions in your code, enabling your programs to respond differently based on various conditions.

3.2.1 Equality (==)

The equality operator checks if two values are equal. If they are, the expression evaluates to True; otherwise, it evaluates to False.

Python

```
result = 5 == 5    # result will be True
result = 10 == 5   # result will be False
```

3.2.2 Inequality (!=)

The inequality operator checks if two values are not equal. If they are different, the expression evaluates to True; otherwise, it evaluates to False.

Python

```
result = 5 != 5   # result will be False
result = 10 != 5  # result will be True
```

3.2.3 Greater Than (>)

The greater than operator checks if the left value is greater than the right value.

Python

```
result = 10 > 5   # result will be True
result = 5 > 10   # result will be False
```

3.2.4 Less Than (<)

The less than operator checks if the left value is less than the right value.

Python

```
result = 5 < 10   # result will be True
result = 10 < 5   # result will be False
```

3.2.5 Greater Than or Equal To (>=)

The greater than or equal to operator checks if the left value is greater than or equal to the right value.

Python

```
result = 10 >= 5   # result will be True
result = 5 >= 10   # result will be False
result = 5 >= 5    # result will be True
```

3.2.6 Less Than or Equal To (<=)

The less than or equal to operator checks if the left value is less than or equal to the right value.

Python

```
result = 5 <= 10   # result will be True
result = 10 <= 5   # result will be False
result = 5 <= 5    # result will be True
```

3.2.7 Comparing Different Data Types

You can use comparison operators to compare values of different data types, but be mindful of the results. For example, comparing a string and a number might not always produce the expected outcome.

3.2.8 Using Comparison Operators in Conditional Statements

Comparison operators are frequently used in conditional statements (like `if` statements) to control the flow of a program based on comparisons.

Python

```python
age = 20
if age >= 18:
    print("You are an adult.")
else:
    print("You are a minor.")
```

In this example, the code checks if the `age` variable is greater than or equal to 18. If it is, the first block of code is executed; otherwise, the second block is executed.

By understanding comparison operators, you gain the ability to create programs that make decisions based on data comparisons, enabling more dynamic and responsive applications.

Logical Operators (and, or, not)

Logical operators allow you to combine multiple comparison expressions to create more complex conditions. They are essential for building programs that make decisions based on multiple factors.

3.3.1 `and` Operator

The `and` operator returns `True` if both the expressions on its left and right sides are `True`. Otherwise, it returns `False`.

Python

```
age = 25
is_student = True

if age >= 18 and is_student:
    print("You are an adult student.")

# Output: You are an adult student.
```

In this example, the code checks if `age` is greater than or equal to 18 **and** `is_student` is `True`. Since both conditions are met, the message is printed.

3.3.2 `or` Operator

The `or` operator returns `True` if at least one of the expressions on its left or right side is `True`. It returns `False` only if both expressions are `False`.

Python

```python
has_coupon = True
is_member = False

if has_coupon or is_member:
  print("You are eligible for a discount.")

# Output: You are eligible for a discount.
```

Here, the code checks if the user `has_coupon` **or** `is_member`. Since `has_coupon` is `True`, the condition is met, and the message is printed.

3.3.3 `not` Operator

The `not` operator negates the value of an expression. If an expression is `True`, `not` makes it `False`, and vice versa.

Python

```
is_raining = False

if not is_raining:
    print("It's a sunny day!")

# Output: It's a sunny day!
```

In this case, `is_raining` is `False`. The `not` operator negates it to `True`, so the condition is met, and the message is printed.

3.3.4 Combining Logical Operators

You can combine multiple logical operators to create even more complex conditions. However, be mindful of the order of operations and use parentheses to ensure clarity and avoid unexpected behavior.

Python

```
age = 25
is_student = True
has_scholarship = False

if (age >= 18 and is_student) or
has_scholarship:
  print("You qualify for the program.")
```

This code checks if the user is an adult student **or** has a scholarship. Parentheses are used to group the `and` condition, ensuring it's evaluated first.

3.3.5 Logical Operators with Non-Boolean Values

While logical operators typically work with boolean values (`True` or `False`), they can also be applied to other data types in Python. In these cases, Python uses "truthiness" and "falsiness" rules to determine how non-boolean values are treated in logical expressions.

By understanding logical operators, you can create programs that make sophisticated decisions based on multiple conditions, leading to more versatile and powerful applications.

Chapter 4: Control Flow with Conditionals

The `if` Statement (Making Decisions)

Imagine you're writing a program to control a robot. You want the robot to move forward if there's no obstacle in front of it, and stop if there is. How would you tell the robot to make this decision? This is where the `if` statement comes in.

The `if` statement is a fundamental control flow tool in Python. It allows your program to execute different blocks of code based on whether a certain condition is true or false. It's like a fork in the road for your program, directing it down different paths depending on the situation.

4.1.1 Basic Structure of an `if` Statement

The basic syntax of an `if` statement looks like this:

Python

```
if condition:
    # Code to execute if the condition is
True
```

- `if` **keyword:** This signals the start of the conditional statement.
- `condition`: This is an expression that evaluates to either `True` or `False`. It can be a comparison expression (using comparison operators like `==`, `!=`, `>`, `<`, `>=`, `<=`) or any other expression that results in a boolean value.
- **Colon (`:`):** This marks the end of the `if` header line.
- **Indented code block:** This is the code that will be executed only if the `condition` is `True`. Indentation is crucial in Python; it defines which statements belong to the `if` block.

4.1.2 Example: Checking for Age Eligibility

Let's see an example of an `if` statement in action:

Python

```python
age = 20

if age >= 18:
  print("You are eligible to vote.")
```

In this code:

1. We assign the value 20 to the variable `age`.
2. The `if` statement checks if `age` is greater than or equal to 18.
3. Since 20 is indeed greater than or equal to 18, the condition is `True`.
4. The code inside the `if` block (the `print` statement) is executed, displaying the message "You are eligible to vote."

4.1.3 The Importance of Indentation

In Python, indentation is not just for aesthetics; it's a crucial part of the syntax. The indented block of code defines which statements are executed if the condition is true.

Python

```python
if age >= 18:
    print("You are an adult.")
    print("You can get a driver's license.")
```

Both `print` statements in this example are indented, so they both belong to the `if` block and will be executed only if `age` is greater than or equal to 18.

4.1.4 `if` Statements with `else` Blocks

Sometimes, you want to execute one block of code if the condition is true and another block if the condition is false. This is where the `else` block comes in.

Python

```
age = 15

if age >= 18:
  print("You are eligible to vote.")
else:
    print("You   are   not   yet   eligible   to
vote.")
```

In this case, since `age` is less than 18, the condition in the `if` statement is `False`. Therefore, the code inside the `else` block is executed, displaying the message "You are not yet eligible to vote."

The `if` statement is a powerful tool for making decisions in your code. By combining it with comparison operators and logical operators, you can create complex conditions and control the flow of your program based on various factors. This allows you to build dynamic applications that respond intelligently to different situations.

The `elif` and `else` Clauses (Handling Multiple Conditions)

The `if` statement is great for making simple decisions, but what if you have more complex scenarios with multiple possible outcomes? That's where the `elif` and `else` clauses come in, allowing you to handle multiple conditions gracefully.

4.2.1 The `elif` Clause: "Else If"

The `elif` clause (short for "else if") lets you check additional conditions if the initial `if` condition is false. You can have multiple `elif` clauses to handle a series of possibilities.

Python

```python
score = 85

if score >= 90:
  print("You got an A!")
elif score >= 80:
  print("You got a B!")
```

```
elif score >= 70:
  print("You got a C!")
elif score >= 60:
  print("You got[1] a D.")
```

In this example, the code first checks if the score is greater than or equal to 90. If it is, it prints "You got an A!" and the rest of the elif clauses are skipped. If the score is not greater than or equal to 90, it moves to the next elif clause and checks if the score is greater than or equal to 80, and so on.

4.2.2 The else Clause: The Catch-All

The else clause provides a fallback option. It executes only if none of the preceding if or elif conditions are true.

Python

```
score = 55

if score >= 90:
  print("You got an A!")
elif score >= 80:
  print("You got a B!")
elif score >= 70:
```

```
  print("You got a C!")
elif score >= 60:
  print("You got a D.")
else:
  print("You$^2$ failed.")
```

In this case, since the `score` is 55, none of the `if` or `elif` conditions are met. Therefore, the code inside the `else` block is executed, printing "You failed."

4.2.3 Order of Evaluation

The conditions in an `if-elif-else` statement are evaluated in order from top to bottom. Once a condition is found to be true, the corresponding code block is executed, and the rest of the statement is skipped.

4.2.4 Using `elif` and `else` for Clarity

Using `elif` and `else` clauses can make your code more organized and readable, especially when dealing with multiple conditions. It provides a clear structure for handling different scenarios and ensures that your program behaves as expected in various situations.

By mastering the `elif` and `else` clauses, you can create programs that make complex decisions and handle a wide range of possibilities, leading to more robust and versatile applications.

Nested Conditionals (Complex Decision Making)

Sometimes, making a decision involves considering multiple factors and conditions. This is where nested conditionals come in handy. Nested conditionals are simply `if` statements placed inside other `if` statements, allowing you to create more intricate decision-making logic.

4.3.1 Structure of Nested Conditionals

A nested conditional looks like this:

Python

```python
if outer_condition:
    # Code to execute if the outer condition
is True
    if inner_condition:
        # Code to execute if both outer and
inner conditions are True
```

```
else:
    # Code to execute if outer condition is
True but inner condition is False
else:
    # Code to execute if the outer condition
is False
```

The key here is that the inner `if-else` statement is only evaluated if the outer `if` condition is true. This allows you to create a hierarchy of conditions, where subsequent decisions depend on previous outcomes.

4.3.2 Example: Checking for Discounts

Let's imagine a store offering discounts based on customer age and membership status:

Python

```python
age = 25
is_member = True

if age >= 18:
    print("You are eligible for adult
discounts.")
    if is_member:
```

```
    print("You get an additional 10% member
discount!")
  else:
      print("Consider becoming a member for
extra savings!")
else:
    print("You are eligible for junior
discounts.")
```

In this code:

1. The outer `if` statement checks if the customer is an adult (`age >= 18`).
2. If they are, the code inside the outer `if` block is executed.
3. This includes another `if` statement (nested conditional) that checks if the customer is a member (`is_member`).
4. If they are a member, they get an additional discount message. Otherwise, they are encouraged to become a member.
5. If the customer is not an adult, the code in the outer `else` block is executed, offering junior discounts.

4.3.3 Multiple Levels of Nesting

You can nest conditionals to multiple levels to handle even more complex scenarios. However, be cautious with excessive nesting, as it can make your code harder to read and maintain.

4.3.4 Alternatives to Nested Conditionals

In some cases, there might be more concise and readable alternatives to nested conditionals, such as using logical operators (`and`, `or`) or refactoring your code into functions.

4.3.5 Using Nested Conditionals Effectively

Nested conditionals are a powerful tool for implementing complex decision-making logic in your programs. By carefully structuring your nested `if` statements, you can create applications that respond intelligently to various situations and user inputs. However, strive for clarity and maintainability by avoiding excessive nesting and considering alternative approaches when appropriate.

Chapter 5: Loops for Repetition

The `for` Loop (Iterating over Sequences)

Imagine you have a basket of apples, and you want to peel each one. You'd pick up an apple, peel it, put it aside, and repeat the process until all the apples are peeled. This repetitive action is what loops are all about in programming.

The `for` loop in Python is designed for iterating over a sequence of items. This sequence could be a list of numbers, a string of characters, or any other iterable object. The loop executes a block of code for each item in the sequence, allowing you to perform the same action on each element.

5.1.1 Basic Structure of a `for` Loop

The basic syntax of a `for` loop looks like this:

Python

```
for item in sequence:
    # Code to execute for each item
```

- `for` **keyword:** This signals the start of the loop.

- `item`: This is a variable that represents the current item being processed in the loop. You can choose any valid variable name here.
- `in` **keyword:** This connects the `item` variable to the `sequence`.
- `sequence`: This is the iterable object you want to loop over (e.g., a list, string, tuple).
- **Colon (`:`):** This marks the end of the `for` header line.
- **Indented code block:** This is the code that will be executed for each item in the sequence.

5.1.2 Example: Printing a List of Names

Let's see a simple example:

Python

```python
names = ["Alice", "Bob", "Charlie"]

for name in names:
    print("Hello, " + name + "!")
```

In this code:

1. We create a list called `names` containing three names.

2. The `for` loop iterates over each `name` in the `names` list.
3. For each `name`, the `print` statement greets the person by name.

This will produce the following output:

```
Hello, Alice!
Hello, Bob!
Hello, Charlie!
```

5.1.3 Iterating Over Strings

You can also use a `for` loop to iterate over the characters in a string:

Python

```
message = "Python"

for letter in message:
  print(letter)
```

This will print each letter of the word "Python" on a separate line.

5.1.4 The `range()` Function

The `range()` function is often used with `for` loops to generate a sequence of numbers.

Python

```
for i in range(5):    # Generates numbers
from 0 to 4
  print(i)
```

This will print the numbers 0, 1, 2, 3, and 4.

5.1.5 Looping with Indices

If you need to access the index (position) of each item in a sequence while looping, you can use the `enumerate()` function:

Python

```
names = ["Alice", "Bob", "Charlie"]

for index, name in enumerate(names):
  print(f"Name {index+1}: {name}")
```

This will print:

```
Name 1: Alice
Name 2: Bob
Name 3: Charlie
```

By understanding the `for` loop and its various applications, you gain a powerful tool for repeating actions and processing sequences of data efficiently. This opens up a wide range of possibilities for automating tasks and working with collections of information in your Python programs.

The `while` Loop (Repeating Based on a Condition)

Imagine a game where you keep playing until you run out of lives. The game continues to loop as long as your lives are greater than zero. This kind of repetition based on a condition is where the `while` loop shines.

Unlike the `for` loop, which iterates over a known sequence, the `while` loop repeats a block of code as long as a given condition remains true. This makes it ideal for situations where you don't know in advance how many times you need to repeat the code.

5.2.1 Basic Structure of a `while` Loop

The basic syntax of a `while` loop looks like this:

Python

```
while condition:
    # Code to execute while the condition is True
```

- `while` **keyword:** This signals the start of the loop.
- `condition`: This is an expression that evaluates to either `True` or `False`. It can be a comparison expression, a boolean variable, or any other expression that results in a boolean value.
- **Colon (`:`):** This marks the end of the `while` header line.
- **Indented code block:** This is the code that will be executed repeatedly as long as the `condition` is `True`.

5.2.2 Example: Counting Down

Let's see a simple countdown example:

Python

```
count = 5

while count > 0:
  print(count)
  count = count - 1

print("Blast off!")
```

In this code:

1. We initialize a variable count to 5.
2. The while loop checks if count is greater than 0.
3. While the condition is true, it prints the current value of count and then decrements count by 1.
4. This continues until count becomes 0, at which point the condition becomes false, and the loop terminates.
5. Finally, "Blast off!" is printed.

5.2.3 Infinite Loops: Proceed with Caution

If the condition in a while loop never becomes false, the loop will run indefinitely, creating an infinite loop. This can cause your program to freeze or crash.

Python

```
# Example of an infinite loop (avoid this!)
while True:
  print("This will print forever...")
```

To avoid infinite loops, make sure that the condition in your `while` loop eventually becomes false. This usually involves modifying a variable within the loop's code block, as we did with the `count` variable in the countdown example.

5.2.4 Using `while` Loops for Input Validation

`while` loops are often used to validate user input, ensuring that the user provides valid data.

Python

```
while True:
  age = int(input("Enter your age (must be
18 or older): "))
  if age >= 18:
    break
  else:
    print("Invalid age. Please try again.")

print("You are old enough.")
```

This code repeatedly asks the user for their age until they enter a value that is 18 or older.

5.2.5 Choosing Between `for` and `while` Loops

Use a `for` loop when you know the number of iterations in advance or need to iterate over a specific sequence. Use a `while` loop when the number of iterations is uncertain and depends on a condition.

By understanding the `while` loop and its applications, you gain a flexible tool for creating repetitive actions in your code. This allows you to build dynamic programs that respond to changing conditions and user interactions.

Loop Control Statements (`break`, `continue`)

Sometimes, you need more fine-grained control over your loops. You might want to exit a loop prematurely if a certain condition is met, or skip over certain iterations. This is where loop control statements like `break` and `continue` come in.

5.3.1 The `break` Statement: Exiting a Loop Prematurely

The `break` statement allows you to exit a loop (either `for` or `while`) before it has finished iterating through all the items. This is useful when you need to terminate the loop based on a specific condition.

Python

```python
numbers = [1, 2, 3, 4, 5, 6, 7, 8, 9, 10]

for number in numbers:
  if number == 5:
    break
  print(number)
```

In this code:

1. The `for` loop iterates through the `numbers` list.
2. For each `number`, it checks if the number is equal to 5.
3. If the number is 5, the `break` statement is executed, and the loop terminates immediately.
4. As a result, only the numbers 1, 2, 3, and 4 are printed.

5.3.2 The `continue` Statement: Skipping an Iteration

The `continue` statement allows you to skip the rest of the current iteration and move on to the next one. This is useful when you want to ignore certain items or conditions within the loop.

Python

```
numbers = [1, 2, 3, 4, 5, 6, 7, 8, 9, 10]

for number in numbers:
    if number % 2 == 0:    # Check if the
number is even
        continue
    print(number)
```

In this code:

1. The `for` loop iterates through the `numbers` list.
2. For each `number`, it checks if the number is divisible by 2 (i.e., even).
3. If the number is even, the `continue` statement is executed, skipping the `print` statement for that number.

4. As a result, only the odd numbers in the list are printed.

5.3.3 Using `break` and `continue` with `while` Loops

You can also use `break` and `continue` statements within `while` loops. This is particularly useful for controlling loops with complex conditions or user input.

Python

```
while True:
    user_input = input("Enter a number (or
'q' to quit): ")
  if user_input == 'q':
    break
  number = int(user_input)
  # ... process the number ...
```

This code repeatedly asks the user for a number until they enter 'q' to quit.

5.3.4 Using `break` and `continue` Wisely

While `break` and `continue` can be helpful, overuse can make your code harder to follow. In many cases, you can achieve the same logic with carefully structured conditions or by refactoring your code into functions.

By understanding loop control statements, you gain more fine-grained control over your loops, allowing you to create more dynamic and responsive programs. However, use them judiciously and strive for clarity in your code.

Part 2: Building Blocks of Programs

Chapter 6: Functions: Organizing Your Code

Defining and Calling Functions

Imagine you're baking a cake. You wouldn't want to write down the entire recipe every time you need to make one, would you? Instead, you'd write it down once and refer to it whenever needed. Functions in programming are similar – they allow you to define a block of code once and reuse it multiple times throughout your program.

Functions are essential for organizing your code, making it more modular, readable, and maintainable. They encapsulate a specific task or set of actions, allowing you to break down complex problems into smaller, more manageable chunks.

6.1.1 Defining a Function: Creating a Recipe

Defining a function is like writing down a recipe. You give it a name, specify the ingredients (inputs), and outline the steps (code) to achieve the desired outcome. The basic syntax for defining a function in Python is:

Python

```
def function_name(parameters):
    """Docstring (optional)"""
    # Code block to be executed
    # ...
    return value (optional)
```

- `def` **keyword:** This indicates the start of a function definition.
- `function_name`: This is the name you give to your function. Choose a descriptive name that reflects the function's purpose.
- `parameters` **(optional):** These are placeholders for values that you can pass into the function when you call it. They act like ingredients in a recipe.
- `docstring` **(optional):** This is a string enclosed in triple quotes (`"""Docstring"""`) that provides a brief description of the function's purpose. It's good practice to include docstrings to document your code.
- **Code block:** This is the indented set of statements that will be executed when the function is called.
- `return` **statement (optional):** This statement specifies the value that the function should return when it's called.

6.1.2 Example: A Greeting Function

Let's define a simple function that greets a user by name:

Python

```python
def greet(name):
    """This function greets the person passed
in as a parameter."""
    print(f"Hello, {name}!")

greet("Alice")  # Calling the function with
the argument "Alice"
```

In this code:

1. We define a function called `greet` that takes one parameter, `name`.
2. The function prints a greeting message using the provided name.
3. We call the function with the argument "Alice", which passes the value "Alice" to the `name` parameter.

This will output:

```
Hello, Alice!
```

6.1.3 Calling a Function: Using the Recipe

Calling a function is like using a recipe. You provide the necessary ingredients (arguments) and the function executes its code block, potentially returning a result. To call a function, simply use its name followed by parentheses and any required arguments:

Python

```
function_name(arguments)
```

6.1.4 Benefits of Using Functions

- **Reusability:** Avoid code duplication by defining a function once and calling it multiple times.
- **Modularity:** Break down complex tasks into smaller, more manageable functions.
- **Readability:** Improve code organization and make it easier to understand.
- **Maintainability:** Simplify debugging and updating code by isolating logic within functions.

By understanding how to define and call functions, you gain a powerful tool for organizing and structuring your code. This leads to more efficient, readable, and maintainable programs.

Function Arguments and Parameters

Let's go back to our cake-baking analogy. A cake recipe might require ingredients like flour, sugar, and eggs. These ingredients are like **parameters** in a function – they specify what kind of data the function expects to receive. When you actually bake the cake, you use specific amounts of these ingredients, like 2 cups of flour, 1 cup of sugar, and 2 eggs. These specific amounts are like **arguments** – the actual values you provide to the function when you call it.

6.2.1 Parameters: Placeholders for Data

Parameters are defined within the function's parentheses during its definition. They act as placeholders or variables that will hold the values passed to the function when it's called.

Python

```
def greet(name, age):    # 'name' and 'age'
are parameters
    print(f"Hello, {name}! You are {age}
years old.")
```

In this example, `name` and `age` are parameters. They don't have specific values yet; they're just placeholders waiting to be filled.

6.2.2 Arguments: Actual Values

Arguments are the actual values you provide to the function when you call it. They are placed within the parentheses during the function call.

Python

```
greet("Alice", 30)    # "Alice" and 30 are
arguments
```

Here, "Alice" is the argument passed to the `name` parameter, and 30 is the argument passed to the `age` parameter.

6.2.3 Positional Arguments: Order Matters

In Python, arguments are typically passed to functions based on their position. This means the first argument is assigned to the first parameter, the second argument to the second parameter, and so on.

Python

```python
def calculate_area(length, width):
  area = length * width
  return area

result = calculate_area(5, 10)   # 5 is
assigned to 'length', 10 to 'width'
print(result)  # Output: 50
```

6.2.4 Keyword Arguments: Clarity with Names

You can also pass arguments using their corresponding parameter names. This is called keyword arguments, and it allows you to pass arguments in any order.

Python

```python
result = calculate_area(width=10, length=5)
# Order doesn't matter here
print(result)  # Output: 50
```

6.2.5 Default Arguments: Providing Fallback Values

You can define default values for parameters in a function. These default values are used if the corresponding argument is not provided during the function call.

Python

```python
def greet(name, greeting="Hello"):    # 'greeting' has a default value
  print(f"{greeting}, {name}!")

greet("Alice")  # Output: Hello, Alice!
greet("Bob", "Hi")  # Output: Hi, Bob!
```

6.2.6 Variable Number of Arguments: Flexibility with *args and **kwargs

Python allows you to define functions that can accept a variable number of arguments using special syntax like *args (for positional arguments) and **kwargs (for keyword arguments). We'll explore these in more detail later in the book.

By understanding how arguments and parameters work, you gain the ability to create flexible and reusable functions that can operate on different data inputs. This is a crucial step towards writing more modular and efficient code.

Return Values and Scope

Functions can not only perform actions but also produce results. Imagine a calculator function that takes two numbers and returns their sum. This "returning" of a result is done using the `return` statement, and it's crucial for making functions versatile and reusable.

6.3.1 The `return` Statement: Sending Back a Result

The `return` statement allows a function to send a value back to the code that called it. This value can be of any data type – a number, a string, a list, or even another function!

Python

```python
def add(x, y):
    """This function adds two numbers and
returns the sum."""
    sum = x + y
    return sum
```

```
result = add(5, 3)   # Calling the function
and storing the result
print(result)   # Output: 8
```

In this example:

1. The `add` function takes two parameters, `x`
   and `y`.
2. It calculates their sum and stores it in the
   `sum` variable.
3. The `return sum` statement sends the value
   of `sum` back to the caller.
4. The `result = add(5, 3)` line calls the
   function and stores the returned value (8) in
   the `result` variable.

6.3.2 Functions without `return` Statements

If a function doesn't have a `return` statement, it
implicitly returns `None`. `None` is a special value in
Python that represents the absence of a value.

6.3.3 Scope: Variable Visibility

Scope refers to the region of your code where a
variable is accessible or visible. Variables defined

inside a function have local scope, meaning they can only be accessed within that function. Variables defined outside any function have global scope, meaning they can be accessed from anywhere in the program.

Python

```python
global_var = 10  # Global variable

def my_function():
    local_var = 5  # Local variable
    print(global_var)   # Can access global variables
    print(local_var)    # Can access local variables

my_function()
print(global_var)    # Can access global variables
print(local_var)    # Error! Cannot access local variables outside the function
```

In this example, global_var is accessible both inside and outside the function. However, local_var is only accessible within my_function.

Trying to access it outside the function will result in an error.

6.3.4 Why Scope Matters

Scope helps prevent naming conflicts and makes your code more organized. By keeping variables within their appropriate scopes, you ensure that they don't interfere with each other and that your code behaves as expected.

6.3.5 Modifying Global Variables within Functions

If you need to modify a global variable from within a function, you need to use the `global` keyword to declare that you're working with the global variable and not creating a new local variable with the same name.

Python

```python
counter = 0

def increment_counter():
  global counter
  counter = counter + 1

increment_counter()
print(counter)   # Output: 1
```

By understanding return values and scope, you can write more effective and modular functions that interact with the rest of your program in a controlled and predictable manner. This is a crucial step towards mastering the art of function design and writing clean, efficient Python code.

Chapter 7: Data Structures: Lists and Tuples

Working with Lists (Creating, Accessing, Modifying)

Imagine you need to store the names of all your friends. You could use separate variables for each name, but that would quickly become cumbersome. Instead, you can use a **list**, which is a versatile data structure in Python that allows you to store an ordered collection of items.

Think of a list as a container that can hold various types of data, like a shopping list that includes items like milk, bread, and eggs. Lists are mutable, meaning you can change their contents after they've been created – add new items, remove existing ones, or modify their order.

7.1.1 Creating Lists: Building Your Container

To create a list in Python, enclose a comma-separated sequence of items within square brackets `[]`.

Python

```
names = ["Alice", "Bob", "Charlie"]
ages = [25, 30, 28]
mixed_list = ["apple", 10, 3.14, True]   #
Lists can hold different data types
```

7.1.2 Accessing Elements: Retrieving Items from the List

You can access individual elements in a list using their **index**, which represents their position in the list. Indices start from 0 for the first element, 1 for the second, and so on.

Python

```
names = ["Alice", "Bob", "Charlie"]
print(names[0])   # Output: Alice
print(names[2])   # Output: Charlie
```

You can also use negative indices to access elements from the end of the list. -1 refers to the last element, -2 to the second-to-last, and so on.

Python

```
print(names[-1])   # Output: Charlie
print(names[-2])   # Output: Bob
```

7.1.3 Modifying Lists: Changing the Contents

Lists are mutable, which means you can change their contents after they've been created.

- **Changing an Element:**

Python

```
names = ["Alice", "Bob", "Charlie"]
names[1] = "David"    # Change the second
element
print(names)   # Output: ["Alice", "David",
"Charlie"]
```

- **Adding Elements:**
  - ○ `append()`: Adds an element to the end of the list.

Python

```
names.append("Emily")
```

```
print(names)    # Output:  ["Alice", "David",
"Charlie", "Emily"]
```

- ○ `insert()`: Inserts an element at a specific index.

Python

```
names.insert(1, "Bob")    # Insert "Bob" at
index 1
print(names)     # Output: ["Alice", "Bob",
"David", "Charlie", "Emily"]
```

- **Removing Elements:**
  - ○ `remove()`: Removes the first occurrence of a specific element.

Python

```
names.remove("David")
print(names)     # Output: ["Alice", "Bob",
"Charlie", "Emily"]
```

- pop(): Removes and returns the element at a specific index (defaults to the last element).

Python

```
removed_name = names.pop(2)   # Remove the
element at index 2 ("Charlie")
print(removed_name)  # Output: Charlie
print(names)    # Output: ["Alice", "Bob",
"Emily"]
```

- del: Removes an element or a slice of elements.

Python

```
del names[0]   # Remove the first element
print(names)   # Output: ["Bob", "Emily"]
```

7.1.4 Other List Operations:

Lists support various other operations like slicing (extracting a portion of the list), concatenation (combining lists), sorting, and more. We'll explore these operations in more detail later in the book.

By understanding how to create, access, and modify lists, you gain a powerful tool for managing collections of data in your Python programs. Lists are versatile and adaptable, making them essential for a wide range of applications, from simple data storage to complex algorithms.

List Methods (append, insert, remove, sort)

Python provides a rich set of built-in methods that make working with lists even more convenient. These methods allow you to perform common operations on lists without writing complex code from scratch.

7.2.1 `append()`: Adding an Element to the End

The `append()` method adds an element to the end of a list. This is useful when you want to dynamically grow your list as your program executes.

Python

```python
fruits = ["apple", "banana"]
fruits.append("orange")
```

```
print(fruits)        #   Output:    ["apple",
"banana", "orange"]
```

7.2.2 `insert()`: **Adding an Element at a Specific Position**

The `insert()` method allows you to add an element at a specific index within the list. This gives you more control over the order of elements in your list.

Python

```
fruits = ["apple", "banana", "orange"]
fruits.insert(1, "grape")  # Insert "grape"
at index 1
print(fruits)  # Output: ["apple", "grape",
"banana", "orange"]
```

7.2.3 `remove()`: **Removing an Element by Value**

The `remove()` method removes the first occurrence of a specific element from the list.

Python

```
fruits = ["apple", "banana", "orange",
"banana"]
fruits.remove("banana")    # Removes the
first "banana"
print(fruits)       # Output:    ["apple",
"orange", "banana"]
```

7.2.4 `sort()`: Sorting the List

The `sort()` method sorts the elements of a list in ascending order (by default). You can also sort in descending order by passing `reverse=True` as an argument.

Python

```
numbers = [3, 1, 4, 1, 5, 9, 2, 6]
numbers.sort()
print(numbers)   # Output: [1, 1, 2, 3, 4,
5, 6, 9]

numbers.sort(reverse=True)
print(numbers)   # Output: [9, 6, 5, 4, 3,
2, 1, 1]
```

7.2.5 Other Useful List Methods

- `pop()`: Removes and returns the element at a specific index (defaults to the last element).
- `count()`: Counts the number of times an element appears in the list.
- `index()`: Returns the index of the first occurrence of an element.
- `reverse()`: Reverses the order of elements in the list.
- `clear()`: Removes all elements from the list.
- `extend()`: Appends all the elements from another iterable to the end of the list.

7.2.6 Method Chaining

Some list methods, like `sort()` and `reverse()`, modify the list in-place and return `None`. This means you can't directly chain them together. However, other methods like `append()` and `insert()` return the modified list, allowing for method chaining.

Python

```
fruits = ["apple", "banana"]
fruits.append("orange").insert(1,  "grape")
# Chaining append() and insert()
print(fruits)  # Output: ["apple", "grape",
"banana", "orange"]
```

By utilizing these built-in list methods, you can perform common list operations efficiently and concisely. This allows you to focus on the logic of your program rather than the low-level details of list manipulation.

Tuples (Immutable Sequences)

Tuples are another essential data structure in Python, similar to lists in that they store an ordered collection of items. However, there's a crucial difference: tuples are **immutable**. This means that once you create a tuple, you cannot change its contents – you can't add, remove, or modify elements.

Think of a tuple as a sealed container, like a box of chocolates where the assortment is fixed. While you can access individual chocolates (elements), you can't change what's inside the box once it's sealed.

7.3.1 Creating Tuples: Sealing the Container

To create a tuple in Python, enclose a comma-separated sequence of items within parentheses ().

Python

```
coordinates = (10, 20)
colors = ("red", "green", "blue")
mixed_tuple = (1, "apple", 3.14)   # Tuples
can hold different data types
```

7.3.2 Accessing Elements: Similar to Lists

Accessing elements in a tuple is done in the same way as lists, using their index within square brackets [].

Python

```
coordinates = (10, 20)
print(coordinates[0])   # Output: 10
print(coordinates[1])   # Output: 20
```

You can also use negative indices to access elements from the end of the tuple, just like with lists.

7.3.3 Immutability: The Key Difference

The key characteristic of tuples is their immutability. This means you cannot modify the elements of a tuple once it's created.

Python

```
coordinates = (10, 20)
coordinates[0] = 30   # This will raise a
TypeError
```

Trying to modify a tuple element will result in a `TypeError`, indicating that tuples do not support item assignment.

7.3.4 Why Use Tuples?

- **Data Integrity:** When you need to ensure that data remains constant throughout your program, tuples provide a safeguard against accidental modification.

- **Performance:** Tuples can be slightly more efficient than lists in terms of memory and performance, especially for large datasets, because Python knows their size and contents won't change.
- **Hashability:** Tuples can be used as keys in dictionaries (which we'll explore later), while lists cannot, because keys need to be immutable.

7.3.5 When to Choose Tuples over Lists

- Use tuples when you have a collection of items that should not be changed after creation.
- Use lists when you need a collection that can be modified dynamically.

7.3.6 Tuple Packing and Unpacking

Python allows you to create tuples without parentheses in some cases, and it also supports a convenient feature called tuple unpacking:

Python

```
# Tuple packing
coordinates = 10, 20    # Creates a tuple
(10, 20)

# Tuple unpacking
```

```
x, y = coordinates   # Assigns 10 to x and
20 to y
```

By understanding tuples and their immutability, you gain another valuable tool for managing data in your Python programs. Tuples offer data integrity and performance advantages in situations where you need to represent a fixed collection of items.

Chapter 8: Data Structures: Dictionaries and Sets

Understanding Dictionaries (Key-Value Pairs)

Think of a real-world dictionary. You use a word (the key) to find its definition (the value). Python dictionaries work similarly. They are incredibly useful for storing data in a way that allows for quick and easy access.

Instead of using numerical indices like lists, dictionaries use **keys** to identify and retrieve associated **values**. This makes them ideal for representing relationships between pieces of information.

8.1.1 Constructing Dictionaries

To create a dictionary, use curly braces {} and separate key-value pairs with colons :.

Python

```
employee_info = {"name": "Alice", "id":
123, "department": "Sales"}
product_inventory = {"apples": 50,
"bananas": 30, "oranges": 75}
```

8.1.2 Keys: The Unique Identifiers

Keys in a dictionary have a few important rules:

- **Uniqueness:** Each key must be unique within a dictionary. You can't have duplicate keys.
- **Immutability:** Keys must be of an immutable data type, such as strings, numbers, or tuples. This ensures that the key remains constant and can be reliably used to access its associated value.

8.1.3 Values: The Information

Values in a dictionary can be of any data type, offering great flexibility. You can store simple values like numbers and strings, or more complex structures like lists and even other dictionaries.

8.1.4 Retrieving Values: Accessing Data

To access a value in a dictionary, use the corresponding key within square brackets `[]`.

Python

```python
employee_name = employee_info["name"]
print(employee_name)   # Output: Alice
```

8.1.5 Modifying Dictionaries: Dynamic Updates

Dictionaries are mutable, allowing you to change their contents after creation.

- **Adding a New Key-Value Pair:**

Python

```python
employee_info["salary"] = 60000   # Adds a
new key-value pair
```

- **Updating an Existing Value:**

Python

```python
product_inventory["apples"] = 65   # Updates
the value associated with "apples"
```

- **Removing a Key-Value Pair:**

Python

```
del employee_info["id"]    # Removes the
key-value pair with the key "id"
```

8.1.6 Why Choose Dictionaries?

- **Speed:** Dictionaries are optimized for fast data retrieval. Looking up a value using its key is very efficient.
- **Structure:** Dictionaries allow you to represent data in a structured manner, using meaningful keys to organize information.
- **Versatility:** The ability to store various data types as values makes dictionaries adaptable to different situations.

By understanding dictionaries and their key-value structure, you gain a powerful tool for managing and accessing data effectively. They are widely used in various applications, from storing user profiles to representing complex data relationships.

Dictionary Methods (keys, values, items)

Python provides several built-in methods that make working with dictionaries more convenient and efficient. These methods allow you to access keys, values, and key-value pairs, providing flexibility in how you interact with dictionary data.

8.2.1 `keys()`: Accessing All Keys

The `keys()` method returns a view object that contains all the keys in the dictionary. This allows you to iterate over the keys or convert them to a list if needed.

Python

```python
student_grades = {"Alice": 90, "Bob": 85, "Charlie": 95}

# Iterating over keys
for name in student_grades.keys():
    print(name)    # Output: Alice, Bob, Charlie

# Converting keys to a list
names_list = list(student_grades.keys())
print(names_list)    # Output: ["Alice", "Bob", "Charlie"]
```

8.2.2 `values()`: Accessing All Values

The `values()` method returns a view object containing all the values in the dictionary. This is useful when you need to work with the values independently of the keys.

Python

```python
grades = student_grades.values()
print(grades)    # Output: dict_values([90,
85, 95])

average_grade = sum(grades) / len(grades)
print(average_grade)  # Output: 90.0
```

8.2.3 `items()`: Accessing Key-Value Pairs

The `items()` method returns a view object containing all the key-value pairs in the dictionary as tuples. This is particularly useful when you need to iterate over both keys and values simultaneously.

Python

```python
for name, grade in student_grades.items():
  print(f"{name} has a grade of {grade}")

# Output:
# Alice has a grade of 90
```

```
# Bob has a grade of 85
# Charlie has a grade of 95
```

8.2.4 Other Useful Dictionary Methods

- `get()`: Retrieves the value associated with a given key. If the key is not found, it returns `None` (or a default value if specified).
- `pop()`: Removes and returns the value associated with a given key.
- `clear()`: Removes all key-value pairs from the dictionary.
- `update()`: Updates the dictionary with key-value pairs from another dictionary or an iterable of key-value pairs.

8.2.5 View Objects: Dynamic Windows into the Dictionary

The objects returned by `keys()`, `values()`, and `items()` are view objects. These objects provide a dynamic view of the dictionary's contents, meaning they reflect any changes made to the dictionary.

Python

```
student_grades = {"Alice": 90, "Bob": 85}
```

```
names = student_grades.keys()
print(names)    # Output: dict_keys(["Alice",
"Bob"])

student_grades["Charlie"] = 95
print(names)    # Output: dict_keys(["Alice",
"Bob", "Charlie"])
```

By utilizing these built-in dictionary methods, you can efficiently access and manipulate dictionary data. This allows you to write cleaner and more concise code when working with key-value pairs.

Working with Sets (Unique Elements)

Imagine you have a bag of marbles, and some of them have the same color. You want to know how many different colors are in the bag. This is where sets come in handy. A set in Python is an unordered collection of unique elements. It's like a bag where you can only have one marble of each color.

Sets are particularly useful when you need to eliminate duplicates from a collection or perform operations like union, intersection, and difference, which we'll explore later.

8.3.1 Creating Sets: Defining Unique Elements

To create a set in Python, enclose a comma-separated sequence of items within curly braces `{}`, or use the `set()` constructor.

Python

```
colors = {"red", "green", "blue", "red"}  #
Duplicates are automatically removed
print(colors)   # Output: {"red", "green",
"blue"}

numbers = set([1, 2, 2, 3, 4, 4, 5])  #
Using the set() constructor
print(numbers)  # Output: {1, 2, 3, 4, 5}
```

8.3.2 Sets are Unordered

Unlike lists and tuples, sets are unordered, meaning the elements are not stored in a specific sequence. You cannot access elements in a set using indices.

8.3.3 Adding and Removing Elements

- `add()`: Adds an element to the set. If the element already exists, nothing happens.

Python

```
colors.add("yellow")
print(colors)    # Output: {"red", "green",
"blue", "yellow"}
```

- `remove()`: Removes a specific element from the set. If the element is not found, it raises a `KeyError`.

Python

```
colors.remove("green")
print(colors)    # Output: {"red", "blue",
"yellow"}
```

- `discard()`: Removes a specific element from the set if it exists. If the element is not found, it does nothing.

Python

```
colors.discard("purple")    # No error even
though "purple" is not in the set
```

8.3.4 Set Operations: Union, Intersection, Difference

Sets support various mathematical set operations:

- **Union (`|` or `union()`):** Returns a new set containing all elements from both sets.

Python

```
set1 = {1, 2, 3}
set2 = {3, 4, 5}
union_set    =    set1    |    set2        #  or
set1.union(set2)
print(union_set)  # Output: {1, 2, 3, 4, 5}
```

- **Intersection (`&` or `intersection()`):** Returns a new set containing only the elements that are common to both sets.

Python

```
intersection_set  =  set1  &  set2    #  or
set1.intersection(set2)
print(intersection_set)  # Output: {3}
```

- **Difference (– or** `difference()`**):** Returns a new set containing elements that are in the first set but not in the second set.

Code snippet

```
difference_set = set1 - set2    # or
set1.difference(set2)
print(difference_set)   # Output: {1, 2}
```

8.3.5 Why Use Sets?

- **Uniqueness:** Sets guarantee that all elements are unique, which is useful for eliminating duplicates.
- **Membership Testing:** Checking if an element exists in a set is very efficient.

By understanding sets and their unique characteristics, you gain another valuable tool for managing data in your Python programs. Sets are particularly useful when dealing with collections where uniqueness and set operations are important.

Chapter 9: Modules and Packages

Importing Modules (Using External Code)

Imagine you're building a house. You wouldn't make every single brick and nail yourself, would you? Instead, you'd use pre-made materials from experts in brick-making and nail-forging. Similarly, in programming, you don't have to write all the code from scratch. You can use **modules**, which are files containing pre-written code for specific tasks.

Modules are like toolboxes filled with specialized functions and variables that you can incorporate into your own programs. This saves you time and effort, allowing you to focus on the unique aspects of your application.

9.1.1 What are Modules?

A module is simply a Python file (with a `.py` extension) that contains definitions of functions, classes, and variables. These definitions can be reused in other Python programs by importing the module.

9.1.2 Why Use Modules?

- **Code Reusability:** Avoid reinventing the wheel by using pre-written code for common tasks.
- **Modularity:** Organize your code into logical units, making it easier to manage and maintain.
- **Namespace Organization:** Prevent naming conflicts by keeping code within separate namespaces.
- **Extensibility:** Expand Python's functionality with specialized tools and libraries.

9.1.3 Importing Modules: The `import` Statement

The `import` statement is used to bring the contents of a module into your current program.

Python

```python
import math

result = math.sqrt(25)   # Using the sqrt()
function from the math module
print(result)   # Output: 5.0
```

In this example:

1. `import math` imports the `math` module, which provides mathematical functions.

2. `math.sqrt(25)` calls the `sqrt()` function from the `math` module to calculate the square root of 25.

9.1.4 Accessing Module Members: Dot Notation

To access functions, classes, or variables defined within a module, use dot notation (`module_name.member_name`).

Python

```
import random

random_number = random.randint(1, 10)   #
Generate a random integer between 1 and 10
print(random_number)
```

9.1.5 Different Ways to Import

- **Importing Specific Members:** You can import specific members from a module using the `from ... import ...` syntax.

Python

```
from math import sqrt, pi
```

```
result = sqrt(25)    # No need to use
math.sqrt()
print(pi)  # Accessing pi directly
```

- **Importing with Aliases:** You can give a
  module a shorter alias using the `as` keyword.

Python

```
import random as rnd

random_number = rnd.randint(1, 10)
```

9.1.6 Exploring the Standard Library

Python comes with a rich collection of modules
called the **standard library**. These modules
provide a wide range of functionalities, from file
handling and networking to data processing and
more.

9.1.7 Third-Party Modules: Expanding the Horizon

Beyond the standard library, there's a vast
ecosystem of third-party modules available through

the Python Package Index (PyPI). These modules offer specialized tools and libraries for various domains, such as web development, data science, machine learning, and more. We'll explore how to install and use these modules in the next section.

By understanding how to import and utilize modules, you unlock a world of pre-written code, saving you time and effort while expanding the capabilities of your Python programs.

Standard Library Modules (math, random, datetime)

Python's standard library is a treasure trove of modules, providing a wide range of functionalities for everyday programming tasks. These modules are like built-in tools that come with Python, ready to be used without any extra installation. Let's explore a few essential modules from the standard library:

9.2.1 `math`: Mathematical Functions and Constants

The `math` module provides a collection of mathematical functions and constants.

- **Mathematical Functions:**

Python

```
import math

result = math.sqrt(25)   # Square root
print(result)  # Output: 5.0

angle = math.radians(45)   # Convert degrees
to radians
print(math.sin(angle))   # Sine function

result = math.log10(100)   # Logarithm base
10
print(result)  # Output: 2.0
```

- **Mathematical Constants:**

Python

```
print(math.pi)   # Pi constant
print(math.e)   # Euler's number
```

9.2.2 `random`: Generating Random Numbers

The `random` module provides functions for generating random numbers, which are essential for various applications like simulations, games, and cryptography.

- **Generating Random Integers:**

Python

```
import random

random_int = random.randint(1, 10)    #
Random integer between 1 and 10 (inclusive)
print(random_int)

random_numbers = random.sample(range(1,
100), 5)    # 5 random numbers between 1 and
99
print(random_numbers)
```

- **Generating Random Floats:**

Python

```
random_float = random.random()    # Random
float between 0.0 and 1.0
print(random_float)
```

- **Other Random Functions:**

Python

```
random.choice(["apple",          "banana",
"orange"])    # Randomly choose an element
from a list
random.shuffle(numbers)    # Shuffle a list
in place
```

9.2.3 `datetime`: Working with Dates and Times

The `datetime` module provides classes for manipulating dates and times.

- **Getting the Current Date and Time:**

Python

```
import datetime

current_datetime = datetime.datetime.now()
print(current_datetime)    # Output: Current
date and time

current_date = datetime.date.today()
print(current_date)    # Output: Current date
```

- **Creating Date and Time Objects:**

Python

```
specific_date = datetime.date(2024, 12, 25)
# Christmas Day 2024
specific_time = datetime.time(10, 30, 0)   #
10:30 AM
```

- **Formatting Dates and Times:**

Python

```
formatted_date = current_date.strftime("%B
%d, %Y")   # December 25, 2024
print(formatted_date)
```

- **Performing Date and Time Calculations:**

Python

```
time_delta = datetime.timedelta(days=7)   #
Create a time difference of 7 days
future_date = current_date + time_delta   #
Calculate a date 7 days from now
print(future_date)
```

These are just a few examples of the many useful modules available in Python's standard library. By exploring and utilizing these modules, you can significantly enhance your programming productivity and efficiency.

Installing External Packages (pip)

While Python's standard library offers a wide range of tools, the real power of Python comes from its vast ecosystem of external packages. These packages are like add-ons created by the Python community, providing specialized functionalities for various domains, such as web development, data science, machine learning, and more.

To install these external packages, you'll use a tool called `pip`, which stands for "Pip Installs Packages." It's like a package manager for Python, allowing you to easily download and install packages from the Python Package Index (PyPI).

9.3.1 What is PyPI?

PyPI (the Python Package Index) is a central repository of thousands of external Python packages. It's like a giant library where developers share their code for others to use.

9.3.2 Installing Packages with `pip`

To install a package from PyPI, use the following command in your terminal or command prompt:

Bash

```
pip install package_name
```

For example, to install the popular `requests` library for making HTTP requests:

Bash

```
pip install requests
```

`pip` will download the package and its dependencies (other packages it relies on) and install them in your Python environment.

9.3.3 Other Useful `pip` Commands

- **Upgrading a Package:**

Bash

```
pip install --upgrade package_name
```

- **Uninstalling a Package:**

Bash

```
pip uninstall package_name
```

- **Listing Installed Packages:**

Bash

```
pip list
```

- **Installing from a Requirements File:**

You can list your project's dependencies in a `requirements.txt` file and install them all at once:

Bash

```
pip install -r requirements.txt
```

9.3.4 Virtual Environments: Isolating Your Projects

It's good practice to use virtual environments to isolate your projects and their dependencies. A virtual environment is like a separate container for your project, preventing conflicts between different projects that might use different versions of the same package.

You can create a virtual environment using the `venv` module (or `virtualenv` for older Python versions):

Bash

```bash
python -m venv my_project_env   # Create a
virtual environment
```

Then, activate the environment before installing packages:

Bash

```bash
# On Windows:
my_project_env\Scripts\activate

# On macOS/Linux:
```

```
source my_project_env/bin/activate
```

9.3.5 Exploring PyPI

You can browse PyPI online to discover new packages and learn about their functionalities. Each package has its own documentation and examples to help you get started.

By mastering `pip` and utilizing external packages, you can significantly expand your Python toolkit and build more sophisticated and powerful applications.

Part 3: Putting It All Together

Chapter 10: Working with Files

Reading from Files

While Python's standard library offers a wide range of tools, the real power of Python comes from its vast ecosystem of external packages. These packages are like add-ons created by the Python community, providing specialized functionalities for various domains, such as web development, data science, machine learning, and more.

To install these external packages, you'll use a tool called `pip`, which stands for "Pip Installs Packages." It's like a package manager for Python, allowing you to easily download and install packages from the Python Package Index (PyPI).

9.3.1 What is PyPI?

PyPI (the Python Package Index) is a central repository of thousands of external Python packages. It's like a giant library where developers share their code for others to use.

9.3.2 Installing Packages with `pip`

To install a package from PyPI, use the following command in your terminal or command prompt:

Bash

```
pip install package_name
```

For example, to install the popular `requests` library for making HTTP requests:

Bash

```
pip install requests
```

`pip` will download the package and its dependencies (other packages it relies on) and install them in your Python environment.

9.3.3 Other Useful `pip` Commands

- **Upgrading a Package:**

Bash

```
pip install --upgrade package_name
```

- **Uninstalling a Package:**

Bash

```
pip uninstall package_name
```

- **Listing Installed Packages:**

Bash

```
pip list
```

- **Installing from a Requirements File:**

You can list your project's dependencies in a `requirements.txt` file and install them all at once:

Bash

```
pip install -r requirements.txt
```

9.3.4 Virtual Environments: Isolating Your Projects

It's good practice to use virtual environments to isolate your projects and their dependencies. A virtual environment is like a separate container for your project, preventing conflicts between different projects that might use different versions of the same package.

You can create a virtual environment using the `venv` module (or `virtualenv` for older Python versions):

Bash

```
python -m venv my_project_env    # Create a
virtual environment
```

Then, activate the environment before installing packages:

Bash

```
# On Windows:
my_project_env\Scripts\activate

# On macOS/Linux:
source my_project_env/bin/activate
```

128

9.3.5 Exploring PyPI

You can browse PyPI online to discover new packages and learn about their functionalities. Each package has its own documentation and examples to help you get started.

By mastering `pip` and utilizing external packages, you can significantly expand your Python toolkit and build more sophisticated and powerful applications.

Writing to Files

In the previous section, we learned how to read data from files. Now, let's explore how to write data to files, allowing you to save information permanently or create new files from scratch.

10.2.1 Opening a File for Writing

To write to a file, you need to open it in write mode (`"w"`) using the `open()` function. This will create a new file if it doesn't exist or overwrite an existing file with the same name.

Python

```python
file = open("my_file.txt", "w")   # Open
"my_file.txt" in write mode
```

10.2.2 The `write()` Method: Adding Content

The `write()` method allows you to write a string to the file.

Python

```
file = open("my_file.txt", "w")
file.write("This is the first line.\n")   #
Write a line with a newline character
file.write("This is the second line.")
file.close()  # Close the file
```

This code will create a file named "my_file.txt" with the following content:

```
This is the first line.
This is the second line.
```

10.2.3 The `with` Statement: Ensuring File Closure

It's crucial to close files after you're done with them to release resources and prevent data corruption.

The `with` statement provides a convenient way to ensure that files are closed automatically, even if errors occur.

Python

```
with open("my_file.txt", "w") as file:
    file.write("This is some text.\n")
    file.write("This is another line.")
# File is automatically closed here
```

10.2.4 Writing Different Data Types

To write data types other than strings (like numbers or lists), you need to convert them to strings first using the `str()` function.

Python

```
numbers = [1, 2, 3, 4, 5]

with open("numbers.txt", "w") as file:
    for number in numbers:
        file.write(str(number) + "\n")
```

10.2.5 Appending to a File

If you want to add content to an existing file without overwriting it, open the file in append mode (`"a"`).

Python

```
with open("my_file.txt", "a") as file:
    file.write("This line is appended to the file.\n")
```

10.2.6 Writing to CSV Files

CSV (Comma Separated Values) files are a common format for storing tabular data. Python's `csv` module provides functionalities for reading and writing CSV files.

Python

```
import csv

data = [["Name", "Age", "City"], ["Alice",
30, "London"], ["Bob", 25, "Paris"]]

with open("data.csv", "w", newline="") as
file:
    writer = csv.writer(file)
```

```
writer.writerows(data)     # Write multiple
rows at once
```

This will create a CSV file named "data.csv" with
the following content:

Code snippet

```
Name,Age,City
Alice,30,London
Bob,25,Paris
```

By mastering the techniques of writing to files, you
can save your data, create new files, and work with
various file formats, enabling your programs to
interact with the file system and persist information
beyond the program's execution.

File Handling Techniques

Beyond the basics of reading and writing, Python
offers a variety of techniques for handling files more
effectively. These techniques allow you to perform

operations like checking for file existence, working with file paths, and handling exceptions.

10.3.1 Checking for File Existence

Before attempting to read or write to a file, it's often wise to check if the file exists. This can prevent errors and allow you to handle different scenarios gracefully.

Python

```
import os

if os.path.exists("my_file.txt"):
  print("The file exists.")
  # ... proceed with file operations ...
else:
  print("The file does not exist.")
  # ... handle the case where the file is
missing ...
```

10.3.2 Working with File Paths

File paths specify the location of a file on your system. Python provides tools for manipulating file paths, such as joining path components, extracting file names, and determining file types.

Python

```python
import os

file_path    =    os.path.join("my_folder",
"my_file.txt")  # Join path components
print(file_path)                #        Output:
my_folder/my_file.txt (or \ on Windows)

file_name = os.path.basename(file_path)   #
Extract the file name
print(file_name)  # Output: my_file.txt

file_extension                              =
os.path.splitext(file_path)[1]    #  Extract
the file extension
print(file_extension)  # Output: .txt
```

10.3.3 Handling Exceptions

File operations can sometimes raise exceptions, such as `FileNotFoundError` (when the file doesn't exist) or `IOError` (for general input/output errors). Using `try-except` blocks allows you to handle these exceptions gracefully and prevent your program from crashing.

Python

```
try:
  with open("my_file.txt", "r") as file:
    # ... file operations ...
except FileNotFoundError:
  print("File not found!")
except IOError:
  print("An error occurred while accessing the file.")
```

10.3.4 Working with Different File Types

While we've focused on text files, Python can also handle various other file types, such as binary files (images, audio, etc.) and compressed files (zip, gzip, etc.). Specialized modules and libraries provide tools for working with these specific file types.

10.3.5 File Handling Best Practices

- **Close Files:** Always close files after you're done with them using `file.close()` or the `with` statement.
- **Handle Exceptions:** Use `try-except` blocks to handle potential file-related errors.
- **Use Relative Paths:** When possible, use relative file paths instead of absolute paths to make your code more portable.
- **Follow Naming Conventions:** Use meaningful file names and follow consistent naming conventions.

By mastering these file handling techniques, you can write more robust and reliable programs that interact with the file system effectively. This allows you to store, retrieve, and manipulate data in various formats, enabling your applications to persist information and work with external resources.

Chapter 11: Error Handling and Debugging

Understanding Exceptions (try, except)

Imagine you're driving a car, and suddenly a tire blows out. You don't want the car to crash, do you? Instead, you'd try to control the car, pull over safely, and handle the situation. Similarly, in programming, unexpected events or errors can occur during the execution of a program.[1] These errors are called **exceptions**, and they can disrupt the normal flow of your program if not handled properly.[2]

Python provides a mechanism called **exception handling** to gracefully deal with these exceptions.[3] The `try` and `except` blocks are the core of this mechanism, allowing you to anticipate potential errors and provide alternative actions or recovery strategies.

11.1.1 What are Exceptions?

Exceptions are events that occur during program execution, signaling that something unexpected or erroneous has happened.[4] They can be caused by various factors, such as:

- **Invalid input:** The user entering incorrect data.
- **File errors:** Trying to access a file that doesn't exist.[5]
- **Network issues:** Problems connecting to a server.
- **Division by zero:** Attempting a mathematically invalid operation.[6]

11.1.2 The `try-except` Block: Catching Exceptions

The `try-except` block allows you to "try" executing a block of code that might raise an exception and "catch" that exception if it occurs.

Python

```python
try:
    # Code that might raise an exception
    result = 10 / 0  # Division by zero
except ZeroDivisionError:[7]
    # Code to handle the exception
    print("Error: Division by zero!")[8]
```

In this example:

1. The code within the `try` block attempts to divide 10 by 0, which will raise a `ZeroDivisionError`.
2. The `except ZeroDivisionError` block specifically catches this type of exception.
3. If the exception occurs, the code within the `except` block is executed, printing an error message.

11.1.3 Handling Multiple Exceptions

You can have multiple `except` blocks to handle different types of exceptions.

Python

```python
try:
    # Code that might raise exceptions
    number = int(input("Enter a number: "))
    result = 10 / number
except ValueError:
    print("Invalid input. Please enter a number.")
except ZeroDivisionError:
    print("Error: Division by zero!")
```

11.1.4 Catching All Exceptions

You can use a generic `except` block (without specifying an exception type) to catch any exception that might occur. However, it's generally better to catch specific exceptions to provide more targeted error handling.

Python

```python
try:
  # Code that might raise exceptions
  # ...
except Exception as e:  # Catch any exception
  print(f"An error occurred: {e}")
```

11.1.5 The `else` Clause: Code for Successful Execution

You can include an `else` clause after the `except` block to specify code that should be executed only if no exceptions occur within the `try` block.

Python

```python
try:
  # Code that might raise exceptions
  # ...
```

```
except SomeException:
  # Handle the exception
  # ...
else:
    # Code to execute if no exceptions
occurred
  # ...
```

11.1.6 The `finally` Clause: Cleanup Code

You can include a `finally` clause after the `try-except` block to specify code that should be executed regardless of whether an exception occurred or not. This is often used for cleanup tasks, such as closing files or releasing resources.

Python

```
try:
  # Code that might raise exceptions
  # ...
except SomeException:
  # Handle the exception
  # ...
finally:
    # Code to execute regardless of
exceptions
  # ...
```

By understanding exceptions and using `try-except` blocks effectively, you can create more robust and reliable programs that gracefully handle errors and prevent unexpected crashes.

Common Error Types

As you embark on your Python programming journey, you're bound to encounter errors along the way. Don't worry, it's a natural part of the learning process! Familiarizing yourself with common error types will help you quickly identify and resolve issues in your code.

Here are some of the most frequent errors you might encounter:

11.2.1 `SyntaxError`: **Grammar Mistakes in Code**

Just like natural languages have grammar rules, programming languages have syntax rules. A `SyntaxError` occurs when your code violates these rules, making it impossible for Python to understand what you're trying to do.

- **Examples:**

- Missing colons at the end of `if`, `elif`, `else`, `for`, `while`, `def` statements.
- Incorrect indentation.
- Mismatched parentheses or brackets.
- Typos in keywords (e.g., `pritn` instead of `print`).

- **How to fix:** Carefully review your code, paying attention to syntax rules and indentation. Use an IDE with syntax highlighting to help spot errors.

11.2.2 `NameError`: **Using an Undefined Variable**

A `NameError` occurs when you try to use a variable that hasn't been defined or is not in the current scope.

- **Examples:**
  - Misspelling a variable name.
  - Using a variable before assigning a value to it.
  - Trying to access a local variable outside its function.
- **How to fix:** Check for typos, ensure variables are defined before use, and be mindful of variable scope.

11.2.3 `TypeError`: **Incompatible Data Types**

A `TypeError` occurs when you perform an operation on a data type that doesn't support that operation or when you pass an argument of the wrong data type to a function.

- **Examples:**
  - Trying to add a string and a number.
  - Calling a method on an object that doesn't have that method.
  - Passing a list to a function that expects a string.
- **How to fix:** Ensure you're using compatible data types and that arguments passed to functions match the expected types.

11.2.4 `ValueError`: Invalid Value for an Operation

A `ValueError` occurs when you provide a value of the correct data type but with an inappropriate value for a specific operation.

- **Examples:**
  - Trying to convert a string that doesn't represent a number to an integer using `int()`.

- ○ Passing a negative number to a function that expects a positive number.
- **How to fix:** Validate inputs to ensure they meet the requirements of the operation or function.

11.2.5 `IndexError`: Accessing an Invalid Index in a Sequence

An `IndexError` occurs when you try to access an element in a list, tuple, or string using an index that is out of range.

- **Examples:**
  - ○ Trying to access the 10th element in a list that has only 5 elements.
  - ○ Using a negative index that goes beyond the beginning of the sequence.
- **How to fix:** Ensure that indices are within the valid range of the sequence.

11.2.6 `KeyError`: Accessing a Non-existent Key in a Dictionary

A `KeyError` occurs when you try to access a value in a dictionary using a key that doesn't exist.

- **Examples:**
  - Misspelling a key name.
  - Trying to access a key that has been removed from the dictionary.
- **How to fix:** Check for typos and ensure the key exists in the dictionary before accessing it.

11.2.7 `ZeroDivisionError`: **Dividing by Zero**

A `ZeroDivisionError` occurs when you try to divide a number by zero, which is mathematically undefined.

- **Examples:**
  - `result = 10 / 0`
- **How to fix:** Check for cases where the divisor might be zero and handle them appropriately.

By recognizing these common error types and understanding their causes, you'll be better equipped to debug your code and resolve issues effectively. Remember, errors are opportunities to learn and improve your programming skills!

Debugging Strategies

Debugging is like detective work. You need to carefully examine the clues (error messages, unexpected behavior) to track down the culprit (the bug in your code) and bring it to justice (fix the error). While it can sometimes be frustrating, debugging is an essential skill for any programmer.

Here are some strategies to help you become a master debugger:

11.3.1 Read the Error Message (Really Read It!)

Error messages are your first line of defense. They often provide valuable information about the type of error, where it occurred, and sometimes even hints about the cause. Don't just glance at the error message; read it carefully and try to understand what it's telling you.

11.3.2 Isolate the Problem

Try to narrow down the source of the error. If your code is long, try commenting out sections or simplifying the logic to see if the error persists. This helps you pinpoint the specific part of the code that's causing the issue.

11.3.3 Print Debugging: Your Trusty `print()` Statements

One of the simplest and most effective debugging techniques is to use `print()` statements to display the values of variables at various points in your code. This helps you track the flow of execution and see how values are changing, revealing unexpected behavior.

Python

```python
def calculate_sum(numbers):
  total = 0
  for number in numbers:
    print(f"Adding {number} to {total}")  # Print debugging
    total = total + number
    print(f"Current total: {total}")  # Print debugging
  return total
```

11.3.4 Use a Debugger

IDEs often come with built-in debuggers that provide more advanced tools for debugging. Debuggers allow you to step through your code line by line, set breakpoints to pause execution at specific points, inspect variable values, and more. Learning to use a debugger can significantly enhance your debugging efficiency.

11.3.5 Rubber Duck Debugging

This technique involves explaining your code, line by line, to an inanimate object (like a rubber duck). The act of verbalizing your code often helps you spot errors or inconsistencies that you might have missed while just reading it.

11.3.6 Test Your Code Frequently

Don't wait until you've written a large chunk of code to start testing. Test your code frequently as you write it, adding small pieces and verifying that they work as expected. This helps you catch errors early on, making them easier to fix.

11.3.7 Take Breaks and Ask for Help

If you're stuck on a bug, sometimes the best thing to do is take a break and come back to it with fresh eyes. If you're still struggling, don't hesitate to ask for help from fellow programmers or online communities.

11.3.8 Learn from Your Mistakes

Every bug you encounter is a learning opportunity. Try to understand why the error occurred and how you fixed it. This will help you avoid similar mistakes in the future and improve your overall coding skills.

Debugging is a crucial skill for any programmer. By using these strategies and developing your debugging mindset, you can effectively track down and resolve errors, making your code more robust and reliable.

Chapter 12: Next Steps in Your Python Journey

Exploring Advanced Topics (Object-Oriented Programming, etc.)

Congratulations! You've made it this far and built a solid foundation in Python programming. But the journey doesn't end here. Python offers a vast landscape of advanced topics waiting to be explored, allowing you to tackle more complex problems and build even more powerful applications.

Here are some key areas to delve into as you continue your Python adventure:

12.1.1 Object-Oriented Programming (OOP)

Object-oriented programming is a powerful paradigm that allows you to structure your code around objects, which are like blueprints for creating instances with their own data and behaviors. OOP concepts like classes, inheritance, encapsulation, and polymorphism can help you write more modular, reusable, and maintainable code.

- **Classes and Objects:** Learn how to define classes (blueprints) and create objects (instances) from those classes.
- **Inheritance:** Understand how to create new classes that inherit properties and behaviors from existing classes.
- **Encapsulation:** Explore how to bundle data and methods within a class, controlling access to internal attributes.
- **Polymorphism:** Learn how to create functions and methods that can operate on different object types.

12.1.2 Data Structures and Algorithms

Data structures and algorithms are fundamental concepts in computer science that help you organize and process data efficiently.

- **Advanced Data Structures:** Explore data structures like linked lists, trees, graphs, and hash tables.
- **Algorithm Analysis:** Learn how to analyze the efficiency of algorithms using Big O notation.
- **Sorting and Searching Algorithms:** Study common sorting algorithms (e.g., bubble sort, merge sort, quicksort) and searching

algorithms (e.g., linear search, binary search).

12.1.3 Decorators

Decorators are a powerful feature in Python that allow you to modify the behavior of functions without changing their core logic. They are often used for tasks like logging, authentication, and caching.

12.1.4 Generators

Generators are special functions that generate a sequence of values on demand, rather than generating all values at once. They are memory-efficient and useful for working with large datasets or streams of data.

12.1.5 Concurrency and Parallelism

Concurrency and parallelism allow you to execute multiple tasks seemingly at the same time, improving the performance of your programs.

- **Threading:** Learn how to use threads to execute multiple tasks concurrently within a single process.
- **Multiprocessing:** Explore how to use multiple processes to execute tasks in

parallel, taking advantage of multi-core processors.

- **Asynchronous Programming:** Learn how to write asynchronous code using `async` and `await` keywords, allowing non-blocking operations and efficient handling of I/O-bound tasks.

12.1.6 Web Development

Python is widely used for web development, thanks to its powerful frameworks like Django and Flask.

- **Django:** A full-featured framework for building complex web applications.
- **Flask:** A lightweight and flexible framework for building smaller web applications and APIs.
- **Web Frameworks Concepts:** Learn about routing, templates, databases, and web security.

12.1.7 Data Science and Machine Learning

Python is a popular language for data science and machine learning, with libraries like NumPy, Pandas, Scikit-learn, and TensorFlow.

- **Data Manipulation and Analysis:** Learn how to use Pandas and NumPy for data manipulation, cleaning, and analysis.
- **Machine Learning Algorithms:** Explore various machine learning algorithms like linear regression, decision trees, and support vector machines.
- **Deep Learning:** Delve into deep learning with libraries like TensorFlow and PyTorch.

12.1.8 GUI Programming

Python offers libraries like Tkinter and PyQt for creating graphical user interfaces (GUIs) for your applications.

This is just a glimpse of the many advanced topics you can explore in Python. The key is to keep learning, experimenting, and building projects to solidify your understanding and expand your skills.

Python Resources and Communities

As you continue your Python journey, you'll find that learning is an ongoing process. The Python community is vibrant and supportive, offering a wealth of resources and opportunities to connect with fellow enthusiasts, ask questions, and share knowledge.

Here are some valuable resources and communities to tap into:

12.2.1 Online Documentation and Tutorials

- **Official Python Documentation:** The official Python website (python.org) provides comprehensive documentation, tutorials, and language references.
- **Real Python:** Real Python (realpython.com) offers in-depth tutorials, articles, and courses covering a wide range of Python topics.
- **W3Schools:** W3Schools ([invalid URL removed]) provides beginner-friendly tutorials and interactive exercises.

12.2.2 Online Courses and Learning Platforms

- **Codecademy:** Codecademy (codecademy.com) offers interactive Python courses for beginners and intermediate learners.
- **Coursera:** Coursera (coursera.org) provides Python courses from top universities and institutions.
- **edX:** edX (edx.org) offers a variety of Python courses, including those focused on specific applications like data science and machine learning.

- **Udemy:** Udemy (udemy.com) hosts a vast collection of Python courses, ranging from beginner to advanced levels.

12.2.3 Community Forums and Q&A Sites

- **Stack Overflow:** Stack Overflow (stackoverflow.com) is a popular Q&A site for programmers, with a large and active Python community.
- **Python Forum:** The official Python forum (python-forum.io) is a place to discuss Python-related topics and seek help from other users.
- **Reddit:** The r/learnpython subreddit is a great place to ask questions, share resources, and connect with other learners.

12.2.4 Local Python User Groups

Many cities and regions have local Python user groups (PUGs) that meet regularly to discuss Python, share experiences, and network with other enthusiasts. Check Meetup (meetup.com) or the Python website for groups in your area.

12.2.5 Conferences and Events

Python conferences and events provide opportunities to learn from experts, connect with other developers, and stay up-to-date with the latest trends. Some popular events include PyCon US, PyCon UK, and EuroPython.

12.2.6 Open-Source Projects

Contributing to open-source projects is a great way to learn from experienced developers, improve your coding skills, and give back to the community. GitHub (github.com) is a popular platform for hosting and collaborating on open-source projects.

12.2.7 Online Communities and Social Media

- **Twitter:** Follow Python experts and organizations on Twitter to stay updated on news and trends.
- **Discord:** Join Python-related Discord servers to chat with other developers and get real-time support.

By actively engaging with these resources and communities, you can accelerate your learning, find solutions to challenges, and become a more proficient Python programmer. Remember, the Python community is vast and welcoming, so don't hesitate to reach out and connect with others on your coding journey.

Building Your Own Projects

Learning Python is like acquiring a set of powerful tools. But the real magic happens when you use those tools to build something of your own. Creating your own projects is where you truly solidify your understanding, apply your skills, and unleash your creativity.

Here's a guide to help you embark on your project-building journey:

12.3.1 Start with Small, Manageable Projects

Don't try to build a complex application right away. Start with small, manageable projects that you can complete in a reasonable amount of time. This allows you to gain confidence, practice your skills, and build momentum.

Some ideas for beginner projects:

- **Simple Games:** Tic-tac-toe, number guessing games, hangman.
- **Utility Scripts:** File organizers, web scrapers, password generators.
- **Data Analysis Projects:** Analyze datasets (e.g., weather data, movie ratings) and create visualizations.

- **Text-Based Adventures:** Create interactive stories with choices and consequences.

12.3.2 Break Down the Project into Smaller Tasks

Once you have a project idea, break it down into smaller, more manageable tasks. This makes the project less overwhelming and allows you to focus on one step at a time.

12.3.3 Plan Your Approach

Before you start coding, think about the overall structure of your project, the data structures you'll use, and the algorithms you'll need. Sketching out a plan or creating a flowchart can help you visualize the logic and identify potential challenges.

12.3.4 Write Clean and Readable Code

As you write your code, focus on clarity and readability. Use meaningful variable names, add comments to explain your logic, and follow consistent formatting conventions. This will make it easier to understand and maintain your code in the future.

12.3.5 Test Your Code Thoroughly

Testing is crucial to ensure your project works as expected. Write test cases to cover different scenarios and edge cases. Use debugging techniques to identify and fix errors.

12.3.6 Use Version Control

Version control systems like Git (github.com) allow you to track changes to your code, collaborate with others, and revert to previous versions if needed. Learning Git is an essential skill for any programmer.

12.3.7 Seek Feedback and Iterate

Don't be afraid to share your projects with others and seek feedback. This can help you identify areas for improvement and learn from different perspectives. Iterate on your project based on feedback, adding new features, and refining existing ones.

12.3.8 Don't Give Up!

Building projects can be challenging, and you might encounter obstacles along the way. Don't get discouraged! Persevere, break down problems into smaller steps, and seek help when needed. The satisfaction of creating something of your own is incredibly rewarding.

12.3.9 Some Project Ideas to Spark Your Imagination

- **Web Applications:** Build a to-do list app, a blog, or an e-commerce site.
- **Data Science Projects:** Analyze social media trends, predict stock prices, or build a recommendation system.
- **Machine Learning Projects:** Create a spam filter, an image recognition system, or a chatbot.
- **Games:** Develop a platformer game, a puzzle game, or a strategy game.
- **Automation Scripts:** Automate repetitive tasks like web scraping, data entry, or system administration.

The possibilities are endless! Choose projects that align with your interests and goals, and let your creativity soar.

By building your own projects, you'll not only solidify your Python skills but also gain valuable experience in problem-solving, critical thinking, and project management. So, go forth, create, and enjoy the journey of bringing your ideas to life with Python!

CONCLUSION

Congratulations, Pythonista!

You've reached the end of this journey through the fundamentals of Python programming, and you should be proud of the progress you've made. From understanding basic syntax and data types to wielding the power of control flow, functions, and data structures, you've acquired a versatile set of tools to bring your ideas to life with code.

But this is just the beginning. The world of Python extends far beyond the foundations we've covered. As you continue your exploration, you'll discover exciting new realms like object-oriented programming, advanced data structures, web development, data science, and machine learning. The possibilities are truly endless!

Key Takeaways

Remember the core principles that will guide you on your ongoing Python journey:

- **Embrace simplicity and readability:** Strive for clear, concise code that is easy to understand and maintain.

- **Practice regularly:** The key to mastery is consistent practice. Write code, experiment, and build projects to solidify your understanding.

- **Engage with the community:** Connect with other Python enthusiasts, seek feedback, and share your knowledge. The Python community is a vast and supportive network that can accelerate your learning and growth.

- **Never stop learning:** Python is a constantly evolving language with new libraries and frameworks emerging all the time. Embrace lifelong learning and stay curious.

The Adventure Continues

As you venture further into the world of Python, remember that programming is not just about writing code; it's about problem-solving, creativity, and building solutions that can make a difference.

So, go forth, explore, and create! Build projects that excite you, tackle challenges that push your boundaries, and contribute to the ever-growing Python ecosystem.

I hope this book has ignited your passion for Python and provided you with a solid foundation to build upon. May your coding journey be filled with discovery, innovation, and endless possibilities.

Happy coding!

DEDICATION

This book is devoted to all the inquisitive thinkers, problem-solvers, and visionaries who think that technology may help create a sustainable future. To the people who put in many hours behind the scenes to develop solutions that improve the efficiency, sustainability, and connectivity of our world. May this work motivate you to continue pushing the boundaries of what is possible, and may it serve as a reminder that every step towards energy efficiency takes us closer to a brighter tomorrow.

I want to express my gratitude to my family and friends for believing in me and the significance of this work, as their constant support and encouragement have been my pillars. This is for everyone who recognizes that growth is based on sustainability and creativity.

DISCLAIMER

This book's content is solely intended for educational and informational purposes. While every attempt has been taken to ensure the correctness and reliability of the information, the author and publisher do not make any claims or warranties on the completeness, accuracy, or reliability of the content. The author's opinions may differ from those or policies of any organization or entity that is referenced.

The information in this book is not meant to be used as expert advice in any specific sector, such as sustainability, technology, or energy efficiency. Before making decisions based on the information presented, readers are urged to consult a professional or carry out independent research.

Any obligations, losses, or damages resulting from the use or use of the material in this book are not the responsibility of the author or publisher. All product names, company names, and trademarks mentioned belong to their respective owners.

CONTENTS

ACKNOWLEDGMENTS

To everyone who helped me along the way when I was writing this book, I want to sincerely thank you.

I want to start by expressing my gratitude to my family and friends for their constant support and faith in me. My strength has always come from their understanding, love, and patience. This job would not have been accomplished without their assistance.

I also want to express my sincere gratitude to the mentors, colleagues, and energy efficiency, technology, and sustainability specialists whose advice and ideas have enhanced the substance of this book. I am fortunate to benefit from their aggregate knowledge, and their commitment to sustainability and innovation never ceases to excite me.

We would especially like to thank the readers who are still pushing the envelope in their industries, breaking rules, and working for a more sustainable and greener future. I hope this book is a little addition to your continued efforts,

1

which are the driving force behind it.

Last but not least, I want to thank the several organizations and experts whose case studies, research, and innovative work have been great resources for this book. I genuinely appreciate how your combined efforts have influenced the discussion around sustainability and energy-efficient computing.

I appreciate everyone's participation in this adventure.

CHAPTER 1

OVERVIEW OF ENERGY-SAVING COMPUTERS

With technology influencing almost every part of our lives in the current digital era, energy-efficient computing is more important than ever. Optimizing energy usage is not just a financial need but also a moral and environmental obligation as enterprises become more and more dependent on information technology (IT). The idea of energy-efficient computing is presented in this chapter, along with the reasons for its adoption and the difficulties that businesses have when putting it into practice.

1.1 Realizing How Important Energy Efficiency Is

Energy-Efficient Computing: Definition and Importance

The design, development, and implementation of computing systems and procedures that reduce power usage while preserving or enhancing performance is known as energy-efficient computing. This entails streamlining operating procedures, software, and hardware to increase productivity while consuming less energy.

Energy-efficient computing is important because it can save operating costs, prolong the life of computer hardware, and lessen its negative effects on the environment. Making sure these systems run effectively has become a top concern for both the public and private sectors due to the growing demand for processing capacity brought on by data centers, cloud computing, and artificial intelligence.

Summary of Energy Use in the Global IT Sector

One of the industries with the fastest rates of electricity use is the worldwide IT sector. Data centers alone were responsible for around 1% of the world's electricity demand in 2022, according to the International Energy Agency (IEA)**. As digital services grow, this percentage is expected to increase dramatically. This increase in energy usage is a result of the development of high-performance computing (HPC), blockchain technologies (like cryptocurrencies), and artificial intelligence.

A few important figures:

- An estimated 200 terawatt-hours (TWh) of power are used annually by data centers.
- **Cloud Computing:** Huge data centers run by major cloud providers like AWS, Google Cloud, and Microsoft Azure need continuous electricity and cooling.
- The total energy burden is increased by millions of laptops, desktop computers, cellphones, and Internet of Things devices.

In light of this tendency, increasing energy efficiency is crucial to controlling the industry's environmental impact and guaranteeing long-term growth.

The Relationship Between Sustainability and IT Energy Use

Sustainability objectives are closely related to energy-efficient computing. Environmentally friendly methods are being pushed on industries as worries about climate change and carbon emissions grow worldwide. Greenhouse gas emissions are a result of the IT industry's dependence on non-renewable energy sources. Data centers, for example, are responsible for about 0.3% of the world's CO_2 emissions, and this percentage is predicted to increase.

Energy-efficient computing has several important advantages for sustainability, including:

- **Reduction in Carbon Footprint**: Organizations can reduce their CO_2 emissions by using less energy.
- **Resource Conservation:** By prolonging hardware life, efficient systems cut down on electronic waste.
- **Alignment with Global Goals:** Programs like the United Nations Sustainable Development Goals (SDGs) highlight the need for responsible consumerism and sustainable infrastructure.

In conclusion, the push for energy-efficient computing

aims to ensure a sustainable future in addition to financial savings.

1.2 Important Factors Influencing Energy-Efficient Computing

Sustainability Objectives and Regulatory Pressures

Regulations to reduce energy use and advance sustainability are being implemented more frequently by governments and international organizations. These regulations include, for example:

- Data centers must report their energy efficiency metrics in accordance with the EU Energy Efficiency Directive.
- **Certification as Energy Star:** A U.S. program that certifies energy-efficient practices and products.
- IT firms are under pressure to lower their carbon footprints as a result of numerous nations' commitments to achieve net-zero emissions by 2050.

Noncompliance with these regulations may result in

penalties, legal action, and operational limitations for certain organizations. Therefore, implementing energy-efficient computing processes is strongly encouraged by regulatory pressure.

Energy Consumption's Financial Effects

A sizable amount of IT operating costs are related to energy. For instance:

- Data Center Power Costs: Typically, 40-50% of a data center's overall operating expenses are related to electricity.
- **Cooling Mechanisms:** A significant quantity of energy is used by cooling infrastructure, sometimes matching or surpassing the power required for computing operations.

Significant cost reductions can result from lowering energy use. For example, businesses can reduce their power costs by 20-30% by using energy-efficient technology and improving server use. A competitive edge can be gained by reinvesting these savings in expansion and innovation.

Public Perception and Corporate Social Responsibility

Businesses that prioritize environmental, social, and governance (ESG) principles are valued more by investors and modern consumers. A company's market share and brand image can be greatly impacted by public opinion. The following are some advantages of implementing energy-efficient practices:

- **Positive Branding:** Businesses with a reputation for sustainability draw in eco-aware clients.
- **Investor Confidence:** A lot of investors favor companies that show a dedication to minimizing their environmental effect.
- **Employee Morale:** Workers are frequently more inclined to work for companies that place a high value on ethical behavior.

In conclusion, implementing energy-efficient computing improves stakeholder trust and company reputation in addition to meeting ethical requirements.

1.3 The Difficulties of Reaching Energy Efficiency

Harmonizing Efficiency and Performance

Finding a balance between energy efficiency and performance is one of the main obstacles to accomplishing it. Real-time data processing, artificial intelligence, and video rendering are examples of high-performance computing applications that frequently demand a large amount of power. Companies need to make sure that:

Efficiency Improvements Do Not Compromise Performance:

- Reducing energy use shouldn't result in a decrease in processing speed or system responsiveness.
- The optimization of hardware: Performance and efficiency can be balanced by purchasing energy-efficient processors, such as ARM-based CPUs or GPUs with superior performance-per-watt ratios.
- **Optimization of Software:** Reducing superfluous computations, using optimized techniques, and

writing efficient code are essential.

The Cost, Technology, and Scalability Trade-offs

Many firms may find it difficult to adopt energy-efficient computing since it frequently requires upfront investments in new technologies. Among the trade-offs are:

- **Upgrade Cost:** Making the switch to energy-efficient cooling or technology may necessitate a large cash investment.
- **Technological Restrictions:** Older systems might not be able to accommodate energy-saving improvements, necessitating replacement.
- It might be difficult to make sure that energy-efficient procedures keep up with the growing computing demands of growing enterprises.

Organizations can address these trade-offs by:

- **Take a Phased Approach:** Replace outdated systems with more energy-efficient ones one at a time.

- **Use Cloud Services:** Make use of cloud providers who place a high priority on infrastructure that uses less energy.

- The Total Cost of Ownership (TCO) should be evaluated. Think about long-term savings instead of just upfront expenses.

Overcoming Change Resistance and Organizational Inertia

One of the main obstacles to adopting energy-efficient measures is frequently changing management. Typical obstacles consist of:

- **IT Staff Reluctance:** Teams may be hesitant to embrace new procedures or systems because they are not well-versed in or at ease using current technologies.

- **Lack of Awareness:** Decision-makers and staff might not completely comprehend the significance of energy-efficient computing.

- Organizations may give short-term objectives precedence over long-term sustainability due to competing priorities.

In order to break through inertia, organizations ought to:

- **Offer Training:** Inform IT personnel on the advantages and methods of energy-efficient computing.
- **Define Specific Objectives:** Set quantifiable goals for energy efficiency and monitor your progress.
- **Incentivize Change:** Provide rewards to groups that successfully adopt energy-saving strategies.

Energy-efficient computing is becoming a global imperative driven by ethical, legal, and commercial considerations rather than just a niche issue. Organizations may create a more sustainable, economical, and responsible IT infrastructure by comprehending its significance, identifying the main motivators, and resolving the issues at hand. Although the path to energy efficiency may be convoluted, the short- and long-term benefits make it an essential endeavor for every progressive business.

CHAPTER 2

IT Organizations' Carbon Footprint

IT companies are becoming major contributors to global carbon emissions as a result of technological advancements and the growth of the digital economy. Data centers, cloud infrastructure, end-user devices, and the manufacturing processes that produce them are all included in the carbon footprint of IT. To make IT more sustainable, it is crucial to comprehend the subtleties of energy usage, find hidden contributors, and put methods in place to lower emissions. This chapter explores various facets with an emphasis on practical knowledge and expert viewpoints.

2.1 Information Technology Energy Use

Energy-Intensive Tasks: Simulations, Rendering, and AI Training

Computing-intensive procedures that need a significant

amount of energy are frequently used in modern IT operations. The following are some of the most energy-intensive activities:

The process of training advanced artificial intelligence (AI) models, especially large-scale neural networks, can use a significant amount of electricity. For instance, it is predicted that training a single GPT-3 model (which contains 175 billion parameters) uses more than 1,287 MWh of energy, which is equal to more than 120 average U.S. houses' yearly electricity use.

Simulations: To design and test goods, industries such as pharmaceuticals, automotive, and aerospace mainly rely on simulations. High-performance computing (HPC) systems that run continuously for long periods of time are necessary for these simulations, especially those that involve fluid dynamics, structural analysis, or molecular modeling.

The production of high-quality visual effects (VFX) and 3D animations for motion pictures or video games in the entertainment sector necessitates extensive rendering procedures. Depending on its complexity, rendering a single frame in a full-length animated movie might take hours or even days, resulting in a substantial overall energy consumption.

Strong processors, GPUs, and enormous data storage systems are required for these energy-intensive processes, all of which have a significant carbon impact. The difficulty lies in striking a balance between energy-efficient methods and these expanding computing demands.

Evaluating the Carbon Footprints of Different IT Operations

Depending on the infrastructure and activity types, IT operations have a wide range of carbon footprints. This is a breakdown of comparisons:

- **Data Centers:** These establishments account for approximately 0.1% of world carbon emissions and 1% of global electricity usage. Data centers use energy for cooling, power distribution, and redundancy systems in addition to processing, and they are always in operation.

- **Cloud Computing:** Cloud services still rely on large data centers that use a lot of energy, even if they combine resources and frequently increase efficiency when compared to on-premises solutions. Although public cloud providers such as **AWS, Microsoft Azure, and Google Cloud** are striving for carbon neutrality, there are still obstacles in areas with a shortage of renewable energy sources.

- **End-User Devices:** The carbon footprint of IT is influenced by laptops, desktop computers, cellphones, and tablets taken together. Even while each of these gadgets uses less power on its own, when combined with the frequent need for updates, replacements, and charging, their widespread use leads to considerable cumulative emissions.

- **Edge Computing:** By placing processing nearer to data sources (such Internet of Things devices), latency can be decreased, but energy consumption may rise as a result of dispersed infrastructure and extra hardware needs.

Organizations can prioritize areas for energy efficiency improvements by being aware of these discrepancies.

Monitoring and Documenting IT Energy Use

A crucial first step in lowering IT's carbon impact is accurately measuring and reporting energy usage. Important procedures consist of:

The ratio of total facility energy to IT equipment energy is measured by Energy Usage Effectiveness (EUE), a statistic that is comparable to Power Usage Effectiveness (PUE). Higher efficiency is indicated by a lower PUE.

Tracking direct and indirect greenhouse gas (GHG) emissions using frameworks like the Greenhouse Gas Protocol is known as "carbon accounting." The following categories apply to emissions:

- **Scope 1:** Direct emissions, such as fuel burning occurring on-site.
- **Scope 2:** Indirect emissions from electricity purchases.

- **Scope 3:** Other indirect emissions (hardware production, supply chain, etc.).

Sustainability Reporting: A lot of companies create yearly sustainability reports detailing their energy usage, carbon emissions, and attempts to reduce them. Guidelines for transparent reporting are provided by organizations such as the Global Reporting Initiative (GRI) and the Sustainability Accounting Standards Board (SASB).

IT firms may uncover inefficiencies and show stakeholders that they are accountable by putting strong measurement methods into place.

2.2 Unknown Factors Affecting the Carbon Footprint

Hardware Manufacturing Indirect Emissions

IT's carbon footprint includes indirect emissions from the production of gear in addition to operational energy use. Important contributors include:

- The extraction of raw materials, such as lithium,

cobalt, and rare earth elements, which are utilized in processors, batteries, and storage devices, comes at a high energy and environmental cost.

- **Manufacturing Processes:** Energy-intensive procedures including lithography, etching, and chemical vapor deposition are used to produce semiconductors, circuit boards, and electronic components. Over the course of their lifetime, the carbon emissions linked to these procedures may surpass the device's operational emissions.

- **Transport and Logistics:** Indirect emissions are increased when hardware components are shipped across international supply chains. Every stage of production adds to the overall carbon footprint due to the need on foreign freight, whether it be by air, sea, or road.

Energy Consumption in Cloud and Data Center Operations

Although data centers are frequently thought of as the

backbone of digital infrastructure, they do have significant energy consumption and emissions. The following are some hidden elements that affect data center carbon footprints:

- **Cooling Systems:** 30-40% of the energy used in a data center can be attributed to cooling. Energy demand is further increased by inefficient cooling systems or those that use conventional air-conditioning techniques.

- **Redundant Systems:** Data centers require redundant infrastructure and backup power sources (such diesel generators) to ensure dependability, which can raise carbon emissions, particularly if the backup power is derived from fossil fuels.

- **Underutilized Servers:** Even when servers are not being used, they still use a lot of electricity. 30% of servers in data centers are thought to be "comatose" running but doing little or no work.

Global IT Supply Chains' Effects

With various continents and a large number of stakeholders, IT supply chains are extremely complicated. The following are important variables affecting these supply chains' carbon footprints:

- The carbon footprint of production facilities is higher in countries with carbon-intensive power grids (such as coal-reliant regions) than in areas with renewable energy.

- **Component Sourcing:** Various parts (such as memory modules, displays, and microchips) are frequently purchased from different vendors, each of which adds to the total footprint.

- **End-of-Life Disposal:** IT hardware that is not properly recycled or disposed of contributes to carbon emissions and environmental contamination. Processing e-waste in poor nations with loose rules may make the problem worse.

IT companies can implement more comprehensive

sustainability policies by being aware of these hidden contributions.

2.3 Methods for Lowering IT Carbon Footprints

Compute-Intensive Application Optimization

Energy consumption can be considerably decreased by increasing the effectiveness of compute-intensive programs. Some strategies are:

- **Algorithmic Efficiency:** The computational burden can be decreased by optimizing code and using more effective algorithms. For instance, AI models can save time and energy by using quantization and pruning.

- **Workload Scheduling:** Efficiency can be increased by allocating workloads to maximize server utilization and planning computation activities for off-peak times.

The use of virtual machines (VMs) and containers to

consolidate workloads can boost server utilization rates and decrease the demand for extra hardware.

Making the Switch to Renewable Energy

One of the best strategies to lower IT carbon footprints is to switch to renewable energy. Among the steps are:

- **Power Purchase Agreements (PPAs):** To guarantee a consistent supply of green energy, organizations can sign agreements to buy renewable energy directly from suppliers.

- **On-Site Renewables:** Data centers and offices can offset energy use and lessen their reliance on the grid by installing solar panels, wind turbines, or other renewable sources.

- Selecting cloud providers that are dedicated to using only renewable energy, such as Google Cloud, AWS, and Microsoft Azure, can help cut down on indirect emissions.

IT Hardware Lifecycle Management

Emissions and waste can be reduced with efficient IT hardware lifecycle management. Some strategies are:

- **Extending Hardware Lifespan:** Hardware life can be extended by upgrading individual components, optimizing software, and performing routine maintenance as opposed to replacing complete systems.

- The implementation of responsible recycling programs guarantees the safe processing of end-of-life hardware and the recovery of materials.

- **Circular Economy Practices:** Reducing the environmental impact of manufacturing and disposal is achieved by using a circular economy approach, in which products are made to be reused, repaired, and recycled.

IT companies' carbon footprint is a complex problem that includes indirect emissions from the manufacturing of hardware, direct energy use, and intricate international supply chains. IT companies may drastically lower their carbon footprints by comprehending the major contributions and putting into practice practical solutions like application optimization, the use of renewable energy, and conscientious hardware management. A dedication to innovation, openness, and sustainability is necessary to meet these objectives and guarantee that the IT industry continues to advance without endangering the future of the world.

CHAPTER 3

IT Applications That Use a Lot of Energy

The need for high-performance computing is still increasing rapidly in today's digital environment. IT applications that require a lot of energy, like media rendering, AI training, and computational optimizations, spur technical advancement but also have high energy expenditures. Reducing these processes' energy usage is essential for achieving sustainability and operational efficiency objectives. This chapter investigates the causes of these applications' high energy use, looks at efficiency techniques now in use, and identifies new approaches to lessen their environmental impact.

3.1 AI Inference and Training

The Reasons AI Training Uses a Lot of Energy

Through work automation, improved decision-making, and

the development of novel products, artificial intelligence (AI) has completely transformed a number of industries. However, there is a significant energy cost associated with these developments, particularly while AI models are being trained. High energy consumption in AI training is mostly caused by the following factors:

1. Large Datasets: Processing enormous datasets, which can comprise millions of samples, is necessary for training complex AI models. The quantity and complexity of these databases determine how much computing power they require to handle.

2. Model Complexity: Convolutional neural networks (CNNs) and transformers are examples of deep learning architectures that have billions of parameters, as do other modern AI models. Billions of calculations are needed to train such huge models, which takes a long time on GPUs or TPUs.

3. Iterative Training Process: To maximize performance, AI models are trained across several epochs, which entails processing the same data again. The entire training process can take days or even weeks to finish, and each epoch uses energy.

4. Hardware Requirements: High-performance hardware, like GPUs, TPUs, and large-scale clusters, are essential for AI training and have high power requirements. These systems use more energy when they are cooled.

Examples of AI Models with Low Energy Consumption

To address these issues, a number of institutions and research groups are investigating AI models that use less energy. Among the examples are:

- **GPT-3 from OpenAI:** Despite the enormous energy footprint of GPT-3, attempts have been made to optimize smaller, task-specific variants of this model in order to lower energy usage.

- **DistilBERT** is a more compact and effective version of Google's BERT (Bidirectional Encoder Representations from Transformers)** that maintains 97% of the accuracy of the original model while achieving 60% faster inference.

- **Meta's OPT (Open Pretrained Transformer):** Meta AI has concentrated on developing replicable and transparent AI models while investigating methods to lower training energy consumption.

These case studies demonstrate how task-specific fine-tuning and effective model architectures can lower energy requirements without compromising performance.

New Frameworks and Resources to Lower AI Energy Consumption

New frameworks and instruments are being developed to address the energy challenges of AI:

- **Sparse Training Techniques:** Techniques like as quantization and pruning decrease the number of active neurons or calculation precision, which results in shorter training times and less energy usage.

- **Energy-Efficient Frameworks:** PyTorch Mobile

and TensorFlow Lite are made to optimize performance and energy economy when deploying lightweight models on mobile devices.

- The development of models that strike a compromise between accuracy and energy usage is encouraged by Green AI concepts.

- **Hardware Innovation:** New hardware, such as NVIDIA's A100 GPUs and Graphcore's IPUs (Intelligence Processing Units), are designed to be energy-efficient for AI workloads.

Organizations can deploy AI sustainably while upholding performance standards by implementing these frameworks and strategies.

3.2 Simulations and Media Rendering

Rendering's Function in Visualization and Entertainment

In fields like design, visualization, and entertainment, rendering is essential. It involves using 3D models to create pictures, animations, or films, which frequently calls for a lot of processing power. Important use cases consist of:

- Rendering millions of frames, each of which can take hours to produce, is necessary to create realistic visual effects (VFX) and animated sequences for motion pictures.

- **Video Games:** Real-time lighting, physics simulations, and high-resolution graphics necessitate ongoing rendering operations while playing.

- **Architectural Visualization:** Architects and clients can see projects before they are constructed by using photorealistic renderings for design concepts and virtual tours.

The necessity to compute intricate relationships between light, shadows, and textures makes rendering energy-intensive and frequently necessitates the use of powerful GPUs and specialized rendering farms.

Improving Sustainability through Rendering Process Optimization

There are various optimization techniques that can be used to lower rendering's energy footprint:

- **Adaptive Sampling:** This technique minimizes needless computations by concentrating computational work on crucial regions of a frame (such as regions with intricate lighting or high detail).

- **Real-Time Ray Tracing:** Compared to more conventional techniques, real-time ray tracing advances, such as those found in NVIDIA RTX technology, offer superior lighting effects with less computing overhead.

- **Efficient Algorithms:** The number of calculations required for high-quality renderings can be decreased by combining algorithms such as path tracing with clever sampling approaches.

- **Hardware Optimization:** Rendering workloads are handled more effectively by modern GPUs. Performance per watt can be increased by using hardware accelerators, such as ray-tracing cores.

Using Cloud-Based Solutions to Increase Simulation Effectiveness

There are various benefits of using cloud-based rendering and simulation services for sustainability:

- **Resource Pooling:** Cloud service providers run sizable, highly efficient data centers. They lessen the need for individual businesses to maintain energy-intensive infrastructure by combining resources.

- **On-Demand Scaling:** By enabling businesses to scale resources up or down in response to demand, cloud systems such as AWS Thinkbox, Google Cloud Rendering, and Microsoft Azure Batch help reduce energy waste.

- **Location-Based Optimization:** Data centers for cloud providers are frequently located in areas with a lot of renewable energy. To lessen their carbon impact, businesses might select data centers that are situated in regions that are powered by hydro, wind, or solar energy.

Businesses can accomplish high-quality graphics and simulations without sacrificing sustainability goals by utilizing cloud technologies.

3.3 Algorithms for Optimization

Computational Optimization's Energy Cost

In domains like engineering, finance, and logistics, where determining the optimal solution to a problem is critical, optimization algorithms are indispensable. These algorithms frequently include:

- **Complex computations:** Millions of computations may be needed to explore large solution spaces in order to solve optimization problems.

- **Iterative Refinement:** Using several iterations, algorithms such as gradient descent or genetic algorithms refine solutions, each of which uses computational resources.

- **Real-Time Requirements:** Real-time optimization is required in sectors like manufacturing and trading, which puts extra strain on hardware.

Running these algorithms can have a significant energy cost, especially for real-time or large-scale applications.

Methods for Simplifying Algorithms

Organizations can use a number of strategies to lessen the energy effect of optimization algorithms:

- **Heuristic Methods:** These methods, such as ant colony optimization or simulated annealing, save computing time by producing near-optimal solutions more quickly than exact methods.

- **Algorithmic Simplification:** Complex problems can be simplified into simpler subproblems to increase computing efficiency and manageability.

- **Parallel Processing:** By dividing computations over several cores or processors, optimization is accelerated and the total energy used per solution is decreased.

Using Distributed Computing to Increase Efficiency

Distributed computing uses a number of devices to work together on optimization problems. Important advantages include:

- By distributing work equally among a group of computers, load balancing makes sure that no one machine becomes a bottleneck, increasing productivity.

- **Scalability:** Distributed systems don't need a single, power-hungry supercomputer to scale up to tackle bigger issues.

- **Fault Tolerance:** Distributed systems can function even in the case of a node failure, minimizing downtime and energy loss.

- Distributed optimization is made possible by frameworks like Apache Spark and Hadoop, which enable businesses to use the combined strength of several nodes to do calculations more quickly and with less energy consumption.

Although they are necessary for innovation, energy-intensive IT applications like media rendering, AI training, and computational optimization have high energy costs. Organizations can lessen their environmental impact by comprehending the elements that lead to this energy usage and implementing tactics like cloud solutions, hardware optimization, and effective algorithms. In addition to reducing climate change, giving sustainability a priority in these high-performance processes improves operational effectiveness and corporate responsibility.

CHAPTER 4

NEW DEVELOPMENTS IN COMPUTER TECHNOLOGY

The increasing need for high-performance computing and data-intensive applications are making it difficult for existing computing paradigms to meet energy efficiency standards. With significant improvements in speed, economy, and sustainability, emerging compute technologies including optical computing, neuromorphic computing, and innovative accelerators are set to completely transform the way computational operations are carried out. This chapter explores the fundamentals, uses, recent advancements, and difficulties related to these revolutionary technologies.

4.1 Computing by Optical

Fundamentals of Optical Computing and Its Advantages in Efficiency

Optical computing, sometimes referred to as photonic computing, computes using light rather than electricity. Optical computing employs photons to transport information, whereas traditional computing depends on electrons moving via transistors. The following are the fundamental ideas of optical computing:

- **Photon-Based Data Transfer:** Unlike electrons, light moves more quickly and with less resistance. Photons reduce latency and heat generation by transmitting data at speeds close to light.

- The capacity of optical devices to encode data using various light wavelengths (a technique known as wavelength division multiplexing) allows them to process numerous data streams at once.

- **Low Heat Generation:** Optical systems require less cooling because photons do not produce heat like electrons do, which increases energy efficiency.

Efficiency Benefits:

- **Decreased Energy Consumption:** When compared to electrical interconnects based on copper, optical interconnects consume a lot less electricity.

- **Higher Bandwidth:** Optical computing is perfect for data-intensive applications since it can reach higher data transmission rates.
- **Scalability:** Because photonic components can be reduced in size without appreciably raising power consumption or heat production, optical systems are more scalable than electronic systems.

Optical computing applications in data processing and artificial intelligence

The energy and performance constraints of tasks related to artificial intelligence and data processing may be addressed by optical computing. Important uses consist of:

- **AI Model Training:** It takes a lot of computing power to train huge neural networks. By speeding up matrix multiplications, a fundamental AI function, optical computing lowers training periods and energy usage.
- **Big Data Analytics:** Compared to conventional CPUs or GPUs, optical processors are faster and more effective at processing large datasets.

- **High-Speed Networking:** To manage enormous volumes of data, data centers employ optical interconnects. Throughput and efficiency can be further increased by putting end-to-end optical processing into practice.

- **Cryptography and Security:** Data security operations can be made more effective by using optical computing to speed up encryption and decryption procedures.

Recent Advancements and Difficulties

Recent Advancements:

- **MIT's Photonic Chips:** Scientists have created photonic chips that can execute calculations at a rate that is noticeably faster than that of electronic chips.

- **Lightmatter and Lightelligence**: These businesses are at the forefront of developing photonic processors for AI applications, offering reduced power consumption and faster computation.

- Combining photonic elements with pre-existing electronic circuits to produce hybrid systems that optimize the advantages of both technologies is known as "integrated photonics."

Difficulties:

- **Complexity of Manufacturing:** Compared to conventional silicon chips, producing dependable and scalable photonic chips remains difficult and expensive.

- **Material Limitations:** It is still difficult to create materials that effectively direct and control light at the microscale.

- **Compatibility**: Photonic and electronic systems must be compatible in order to integrate optical computing with the current digital infrastructure.

4.2 Computing that is Neuromorphic

Using Human Brain Models to Increase Productivity

The goal of neuromorphic computing is to provide more effective and adaptable processing by taking inspiration from the structure of the human brain. spiking neural networks (SNNs) are used in neuromorphic systems, which closely resemble the synaptic activity of real neurons, in contrast to traditional von Neumann architectures that divide memory and processing.

Basis Principles:

- **Event-Driven Processing:** Neuromorphic computers reduce idle power usage by activating only in response to data inputs (spikes), as opposed to typical processors that run continuously.

- The ability of neuromorphic systems to process many signals at once, like to the brain, allows for faster and more effective calculations.

- These systems are appropriate for dynamic and changing datasets because of their real-time learning and adaptation capabilities.

Specialized Uses: IoT and Edge AI

In settings where real-time decision-making and low power consumption are essential, neuromorphic computing performs exceptionally well. Important uses consist of:

- **Edge AI:** The low power and latency of neuromorphic processors make it advantageous to deploy AI models on edge devices (such as smartphones, sensors, and cameras). Applications like robotics, driverless cars, and smart homes require this.

- **Internet of Things (IoT):** A lot of IoT devices run on a small amount of power. Neuromorphic chips allow for effective pattern recognition and data processing without the need for frequent battery changes.

- **Sensor Networks:** Neuromorphic processors can interpret data from sensor networks in real-time, delivering quick insights with less energy consumption in domains such as healthcare and environmental monitoring.

- **Robotics:** Neuromorphic systems improve real-time responses and adaptability by enabling robots to process sensory data (sound, touch, and vision) efficiently.

Market Patterns and Anticipated Innovations

Market Trends:

- **Increasing Investment:** Big investments are being

made in neuromorphic research and commercial applications by companies such as Intel (with Loihi), IBM (with TrueNorth), and BrainChip (with Akida).

- Neuromorphic solutions are being investigated by the automotive and consumer electronics industries for use in augmented reality, smart wearables, and autonomous driving.

Anticipated Advancements:

- **Hybrid Systems:** Using neuromorphic processors in conjunction with conventional CPUs and GPUs for jobs that demand both high accuracy and great efficiency.

- **Enhanced Algorithms:** Neuromorphic systems will become more adaptable and able to manage challenging tasks thanks to developments in spiking neural network algorithms.

- **Scalability:** Neuromorphic chips will be more widely applicable when efforts are made to scale them to accommodate more neurons and larger datasets.

4.3 New Speeding Up

Energy-Saving Accelerators for Particular Jobs

Compared to general-purpose processors, specialized accelerators are made to do particular computational tasks more effectively. These accelerators optimize hardware for specific tasks, hence lowering energy usage. Important categories of new accelerators include of:

- The Google-developed Tensor Processing Units (TPUs) are designed to do AI tasks, particularly matrix multiplications in neural networks.
- **Field-Programmable Gate Arrays (FPGAs):** FPGAs provide flexibility and efficiency by being able to be adjusted for particular applications, such image processing or encryption.
- **Application-Specific Integrated Circuits (ASICs):** ASICs are specially made for particular uses, such video encoding or Bitcoin mining, and offer the highest efficiency for those jobs.

Important Figures and Developments in the Industry

Innovation in the accelerator arena is being driven by a number of organizations:

- **Google:** TPUs have established new benchmarks for the efficiency of AI model inference and training.
- In addition to its GPUs, NVIDIA also creates specialized accelerators for edge AI, such as the Jetson series.
- **Intel:** Provides FPGAs for specialized workloads and Habana Gaudi accelerators for deep learning.
- **AMD:** Creates accelerators specifically for AI and high-performance computing, and competes with NVIDIA in the GPU industry.

New Developments:
- **Graphcore's IPUs (Intelligence computing Units):** Specifically engineered for artificial intelligence, IPUs manage parallel computing with exceptional energy efficiency.
- **The Wafer-Scale Engine from Cerebras Systems:** An enormous deep learning processor that offers large-scale AI models previously unheard-of

performance.

Long-Term Effects on Sustainability and IT

The IT sector and sustainability are affected in a number of ways by the use of innovative accelerators:

- **Energy Efficiency Gains:** Organizations can lower overall power usage and enhance performance-per-watt metrics by shifting tasks to specialized hardware.
- **Lower Operational Costs:** Effective accelerators lower the demand for infrastructure, cooling, and electricity.
- **Sustainable Data Centers:** By lowering their carbon footprint, accelerators can help data centers meet corporate sustainability objectives.
- **Democratization of AI:** More organizations, including researchers and startups, may now access powerful computing at affordable prices because of energy-efficient accelerators.

The IT landscape is expected to change as a result of

emerging computational technologies like optical computing, neuromorphic computing, and innovative accelerators. Through the resolution of conventional computing's shortcomings, these advances hold promise for notable improvements in speed, efficiency, and sustainability. The next generation of AI, data processing, and edge computing applications will be made possible by these technologies as they develop, and they will also be essential in lowering the carbon footprint of IT operations.

CHAPTER 5

THE FUNCTION OF DATA CENTERS IN SUSTAINABILITY

Data centers serve as the foundation for contemporary computer infrastructure as the digital world grows. The digital economy depends on data centers for everything from social media and cloud services to machine learning and real-time analytics. However, there are environmental issues and substantial energy consumption associated with these facilities' quick expansion. Achieving sustainable operations in data centers requires an understanding of the energy burden, adoption of innovations, and constant efficiency improvement. This chapter examines green ideas, data center energy challenges, and efficiency measurement and improvement techniques.

5.1 Data Centers' Energy Burden

Recognizing the Range of Data Center Energy Use

One of the buildings that uses the most energy worldwide is a data center. Large amounts of energy are required to run servers, storage devices, networking hardware, and cooling systems. Data centers are responsible for about 1% of the world's electricity demand, according to the International Energy Agency (IEA). This number may be substantially higher in areas with dense data center clusters.

The following are major causes of this energy consumption:

- **Servers:** The main energy consumer, servers require constant power to run around-the-clock. Particularly energy-intensive are high-performance servers used for analytics, AI, and cloud computing.
- **Networking Equipment:** Switches, routers, and other networking equipment use a lot of electricity and help transmit data.
- **Cooling Systems:** To avoid overheating, ideal temperatures must be maintained. Conventional air-cooling systems use a lot of energy.
- **Storage Devices:** Solid-state drives (SSDs) and hard

disk drives (HDDs) need continuous electricity to store and retrieve data.

Traditional Cooling Systems' Effects on the Environment

Since too much heat can damage equipment and cause malfunctions, cooling systems are essential to data center operations. However, conventional cooling systems are very energy-intensive and have detrimental effects on the environment, particularly those that rely on air conditioning and chiller-based HVAC (Heating, Ventilation, and Air Conditioning):

- **High Energy Consumption:** Up to 40% of a data center's energy consumption may be attributed to cooling.
- **Refrigerant Use:** Hydrofluorocarbons (HFCs), which are strong greenhouse gases, are among the refrigerants used in many cooling systems.
- **Water Usage:** Water-cooled systems use a lot of water, which could put a strain on nearby water supplies.

- **Heat wasting:** A common source of inefficiency is the wasting of excess heat produced during cooling.

Difficulties with Legacy Infrastructure Optimization

Because they were constructed before contemporary efficiency standards, legacy data centers present particular sustainability challenges.

- **Outdated Equipment:** In comparison to their contemporary counterparts, older servers and cooling systems use less energy.
- **Inefficient Layouts:** Data center layouts that are poorly thought out might hinder airflow and raise cooling needs.
- **Scalability Issues:** Legacy infrastructures frequently have trouble scaling effectively, which results in energy waste and underutilization.
- **Financial Constraints:** All firms may not be able to afford the substantial investment needed to upgrade or retrofit existing data centers.

Businesses must balance the advantages and disadvantages

of updating old infrastructure in order to meet sustainability targets and preserve operational effectiveness.

5.2 Green Data Center Innovations

Modern HVAC Systems and Liquid Cooling

Data center efficiency is changing as a result of cooling system innovations. Two significant innovations are liquid cooling and sophisticated HVAC technologies:

Liquid Cooling: This method absorbs and transfers heat directly from components using water or specific coolants rather than using air to dissipate heat. Among the varieties of liquid cooling are:

- **Direct-to-Chip Cooling:** Coolant is sent straight to the parts that produce heat, like CPUs and GPUs.
- **Immersion Cooling:** This method transfers heat very effectively by immersing servers in non-conductive cooling fluids.

The advantages of liquid cooling include a 30% reduction

in energy consumption as compared to conventional air-cooling systems.

- By effectively controlling heat, higher-density server racks are made possible.
- Reduces the need for outside HVAC systems, saving space and energy.

Advanced HVAC Systems: Among the innovations in HVAC are:

- **Adiabatic Cooling:** This method uses water evaporation to cool air, which uses less energy than conventional chillers.
- **Free Cooling:** Reduces the requirement for mechanical cooling by using cold regions or outdoor air to cool data centers.

Data Center Energy Optimization using AI

Data centers are using artificial intelligence (AI) more and more to maximize energy efficiency. Large volumes of operational data are analyzed by AI systems to provide forecast recommendations and real-time modifications. Important uses consist of:

- **Dynamic Load Balancing**: AI divides up workloads among servers to reduce heat production and maximize energy use.

- **Predictive Maintenance:** AI models predict equipment breakdowns in advance, minimizing unscheduled downtime and increasing productivity.

- **Temperature Control:** AI-driven climate control systems are able to adjust cooling parameters to maintain ideal temperatures while using the least amount of energy.

Case Study: By implementing AI in its data centers, Google's DeepMind was able to reduce cooling energy use by 40%.

Data Centers Powered by Renewable Energy

One of the main components of green data center activities is the switch to renewable energy sources. Businesses are increasingly using hydro, wind, and solar energy to power their operations. Important tactics consist of:

- Installing wind turbines or solar panels on data center campuses directly to provide clean energy is known as "on-site renewable generation."

- **Power Purchase Agreements (PPAs):** Long-term agreements with suppliers of renewable energy to guarantee a consistent flow of environmentally friendly electricity.

- Data center energy use can be compensated by funding initiatives that lower carbon emissions.

Leading Examples:

- **Microsoft:** By 2025, the company wants to run its data centers entirely on renewable energy.

- **Amazon Web Services (AWS):** Dedicated to reaching carbon emissions that are zero by 2040.

5.3 Assessing and Enhancing Data Center Performance

Metrics: Power Usage Effectiveness (PUE) and Other Measures

Enhancing data center sustainability requires effective efficiency measurement. Power Usage Effectiveness (PUE) is the most often used metric and is computed as follows:

The formula

PUE = Total Facility Energy / IT Equipment Energy

- **Ideal PUE:** A PUE score of 1.0 is ideal, meaning that all of the facility's energy is used directly to power IT equipment.
- **Typical PUE Values:** PUE values in modern data centers are usually in the range of 1.2 to 1.5. PUE values for older facilities may be higher than 2.0.

Although PUE is useful, additional measures are also employed to obtain a more complete picture of efficiency:

- **Water Usage Effectiveness (WUE):** Calculates the amount of water utilized for every unit of energy.
- Data center operations' carbon footprint is measured by the Carbon Usage Effectiveness (CUE) metric.
- A measure of the efficiency with which IT resources are being used is the IT Equipment Utilization Rate.

Case Studies and Benchmarking Instruments

By comparing their data centers to industry norms, businesses can find areas for development with the aid of benchmarking tools. Among the often used tools are:

- **Energy Star Portfolio Manager:** Offers data center performance monitoring and benchmarking.
- The Data Center Maturity Model (DCMM) from Green Grid provides a framework for evaluating data center efficiency in a number of different ways.

Case Study: Using free cooling, effective hardware, and creative design, Facebook's Prineville Data Center was able to attain a PUE of 1.08.

Techniques for Ongoing Enhancement

Data centers can use the following tactics to attain continuous efficiency improvements:

- To find inefficiencies and monitor changes, conduct energy audits on a regular basis.
- **Upgrading Infrastructure:** Switch out old servers,

storage, and networking equipment with more energy-efficient models.

- Reduce energy usage by consolidating workloads onto fewer physical servers through the use of server virtualization.

- **Heat Recovery:** Recover data center waste heat and use it to heat adjacent structures.

- **Employee Training:** Train employees on energy-efficient operations best practices.

Although data centers are essential to the digital economy, their high energy requirements present environmental problems. Data centers may drastically lower their carbon footprint by comprehending their energy burden, applying efficient measures and tactics, and embracing cutting-edge technology like liquid cooling, AI optimization, and renewable power. Sustainable data center practices will be essential to reaching global energy and climate targets as the industry innovates further.

CHAPTER 6

ENERGY-EFFICIENT HARDWARE DESIGN

Hardware design has come under scrutiny for its influence in energy usage as the demand for computational power increases dramatically. A company's carbon footprint is greatly increased by the massive energy consumption of modern computer systems, which range from servers and data centers to Internet of Things devices and edge applications. Energy-efficient hardware design is crucial to reducing this effect. This chapter examines low-power technology advancements, lifecycle management techniques that lessen environmental effect and advance sustainability, and the role of hardware in energy usage.

6.1 Hardware's Contribution to Energy Use

Important Hardware Elements That Affect Energy Consumption

A key factor in determining the total energy consumption of computer systems is hardware efficiency. This energy profile is influenced by several important factors:

- **Central Processing Units (CPUs):** The mainstay of general-purpose computing, CPUs use a lot of energy, particularly in high-performance applications like cloud computing, artificial intelligence, and data processing. In order to minimize energy consumption during idle times, modern CPUs are built with low-power states and dynamic frequency scaling.

- **Graphics Processing Units (GPUs):** AI training, simulations, and rendering are all made possible by GPUs' exceptional performance in parallel processing workloads. However, because of their fast processing speed and several cores, they consume a lot of electricity.

- **TPUs, or tensor processing units, are:** Compared to conventional CPUs and GPUs, TPUs provide faster and more effective performance for machine learning tasks. For AI tasks, their unique architecture dramatically lowers energy consumption.

- **Memory (RAM):** Memory modules use energy when they are not in use. Despite being essential for performance, high-capacity RAM uses more power to preserve data integrity.

- **Storage Devices:** Solid-State Drives (SSDs) are more energy-efficient since they don't have any moving components, whereas traditional Hard Disk Drives (HDDs) use more energy because of their mechanical movement. SSDs, on the other hand, constantly use energy to preserve data integrity.

- **Networking Equipment:** Although routers, switches, and other networking equipment are essential for data transmission, their continuous operation and requirement for high data throughput make them energy-intensive.

Performance and Power Efficiency Trade-offs

Performance and power efficiency must frequently be balanced while designing technology that uses less energy. Important trade-offs consist of:

- **Clock Speed vs. Power Consumption:** Accelerating CPU and GPU clock speeds improves performance but also raises power usage. Dynamic Voltage and Frequency Scaling (DVFS) is a technique used by modern processors to modify clock rates in response to workload demands.

- **Core Count vs. Thermal Output**: Although multi-core processors produce more heat, they perform better in parallel activities. Effective thermal control is necessary to avoid wasting energy on excessive cooling.

- **Latency vs. Efficiency:** Faster access lowers latency but may result in increased power consumption in memory and storage devices. Designers have to maximize efficiency without compromising essential performance requirements.

Reducing precision (for example, from 32-bit floating-point to 16-bit) can save power consumption in AI applications without sacrificing usable accuracy.

Creating Modular and Recyclable Designs

Modularity and recyclability are included into sustainable hardware design to cut down on resource and energy waste:

- **Modular Components:** Hardware changes can be made without replacing complete systems by designing systems with upgradeable and replaceable parts (such as processors, memory, and storage).

- The environmental impact of abandoned hardware is lessened when recyclable materials are used, such as metals and plastics.

- **Design for Disassembly:** Hardware that is simple to disassemble allows for the effective collection and recycling of precious resources like copper, gold, and rare earth metals.

Organizations may prolong hardware life, cut waste, and advance a more sustainable IT infrastructure by giving modularity and recyclability top priority.

6.2 Low-Power Hardware Innovations

Developments in TPUs, GPUs, and Processors

Significant progress is being made by hardware makers in creating processors, GPUs, and TPUs that use less energy. The goal of these developments is to lower power usage without sacrificing functionality.

- **Processors:** Current CPUs, including AMD's Ryzen 7000 series and Intel's Alder Lake, feature hybrid architectures that mix energy-efficient cores with high-performance cores. By allocating activities according to workload needs, this design enables systems to conserve power during low-demand operations.

- Leading GPU manufacturers, such as NVIDIA and

AMD, are concentrating on lowering power consumption using dynamic power management and advanced lithography processes, such as 5nm and 7nm. The Ada Lovelace architecture from NVIDIA optimizes power consumption through AI-based methods.

- **TPUs:** Google's TPUs are made for machine learning applications that require less power and high efficiency. The most recent TPUs use matrix multiplication optimizations and quantization to minimize energy consumption during AI inference.

Customized Hardware for Internet of Things and Edge Uses

Specialized hardware that strikes a compromise between minimal power consumption and sufficient processing capability is needed for edge computing and Internet of Things devices. Examples of innovations are:

- **System-on-Chip (SoC) Designs and Microcontrollers**: ARM Cortex-M series and

RISC-V-based chips are examples of low-power microcontrollers that are made for energy-efficient Internet of Things applications.

- **Edge AI Accelerators:** These devices, such as Google's Coral Edge TPU and Intel's Movidius VPU, enable AI processing at the edge with low energy consumption.

- **Energy Harvesting Devices:** Some Internet of Things sensors are made to collect energy from the surroundings, such as thermal, vibrational, or solar energy, which eliminates the need for wired power sources or batteries.

Memory and Storage Options That Use Less Energy

Innovations in memory and storage are essential for lowering hardware energy usage:

- Low-Power DDR (LPDDR) memory is a type of DDR memory that uses a lot less power than regular DDR memory. It is intended for embedded and mobile applications.

- **Non-Volatile Memory (NVM):** Unlike conventional DRAM, technologies such as MRAM (Magnetoresistive RAM) and ReRAM (Resistive RAM) provide higher speeds and reduced energy consumption.

- **Energy-Efficient SSDs:** NVMe (Non-Volatile Memory Express) interfaces are used by modern SSDs to transport data more quickly and efficiently.

These energy-efficient technologies can be used to help enterprises create hardware systems that support sustainability objectives.

6.3 Hardware Lifecycle Management

Increasing Hardware Life With Upkeep

Hardware longevity lessens the need for regular replacements and its negative effects on the environment. Among the best maintenance techniques are:

- Frequent firmware and software updates lower the danger of early obsolescence and guarantee optimal performance and security.

- **Cleaning and Cooling Management:** Dust accumulation can result in overheating and energy inefficiency, thus it's important to regularly clean hardware components.

- **Monitoring Performance:** Proactive maintenance and early intervention are made possible by the use of diagnostic instruments to track the health of hardware.

Eco-Friendly Recycling and Disposal Methods

Hardware recycling and proper disposal stop hazardous e-waste and make it possible to recover valuable materials:

- Assuring that hardware is disposed of in an environmentally friendly way is possible by collaborating with certified e-waste recyclers.

- **Data Sanitization:** To safeguard sensitive data, devices must be safely cleaned before recycling.

- **Take-Back Programs:** To recycle outdated hardware, a number of manufacturers, including Apple and Dell, have take-back programs.

Using the Circular Economy Principles to Reduce E-Waste

The goal of a circular economy strategy is to maximize resource usage and minimize waste. Among the fundamental ideas are:

- The demand for new products is decreased when hardware is refurbished and resold, extending its useful life.
- Reusing outdated hardware components for new purposes (such as repurposing obsolete servers for low-demand jobs) is known as "upcycling."
- Designing hardware with the goal of reusing materials in future products is known as "closed-loop manufacturing."

Businesses may drastically cut down on e-waste and encourage a more sustainable hardware lifecycle by implementing the concepts of the circular economy.

An essential component of sustainable IT operations is energy-efficient hardware design. Organizations can lower their energy use and environmental impact by using efficient lifecycle management techniques, utilizing low-power innovations, and comprehending the function of critical components. Setting energy-efficient hardware design as a top priority will be crucial to achieving global sustainability goals as technology develops.

CHAPTER 7

SOFTWARE'S CONTRIBUTION TO ENERGY EFFICIENCY

The energy consumption of computing systems is increasing across industries, therefore adopting sustainable software techniques is essential to lessening the impact on the environment. Software is essential to optimizing energy efficiency, even though hardware design provides the framework for it. Developers can reduce the overall carbon footprint and save a lot of energy by optimizing how software uses hardware resources. In order to produce high-performance, sustainable software, this chapter examines optimization strategies, energy-efficient coding methods, and green software development methodologies.

7.1 Techniques for Energy-Efficient Coding

The foundational elements of coding are the first step towards creating efficient software. Developers must carefully analyze how algorithms and processes use computational resources while writing code that is energy-efficient. The best approaches for creating lightweight code, cutting out pointless calculations, and utilizing tools to profile energy consumption are examined in this section.

Creating Lightweight Code and Effective Algorithms

Software analyzes information according to algorithms, and algorithm efficiency has a direct impact on energy usage. Performance can be enhanced and power consumption decreased by developers by choosing or creating algorithms that minimize computational complexity.

Important Guidelines for Effective Algorithms:

- Reducing the complexity of algorithms: Whenever feasible, choose algorithms with a lower time complexity (such as $O(n)$ rather than $O(n^2)$). For sorting activities, for instance, using a linear search instead of a nested loop saves electricity and processing time.

- **Use Appropriate Data Structures:** Operations can be streamlined by using the appropriate data structures. For instance, in certain application circumstances, hash tables offer faster lookups than arrays, eliminating the need for repeated calculations.

- **Avoid Redundant Processing:** Use memoization or caching to get rid of pointless computations. This method saves energy and minimizes repetitive labor.

For instance:

Ineffective strategy:
PYTHON CODE:

```python
for i in range(1000000):
    result = expensive_computation(i)
    print(result)
```

Effective strategy using memorization:

```python
cache = {}
for i in range(1000000):
```

```
if i not in cache:
    cache[i] = expensive_computation(i)
print(cache[i])
```

Reducing Pointless Calculations

Energy is wasted by pointless calculations, particularly in large-scale applications. Code should be closely examined by developers for areas where execution might be made more efficient.

Methods to Reduce Calculations:

- **Lazy Evaluation:** Postpone calculations until the outcome is truly required. This eliminates needless computations, particularly in streaming applications or big datasets.

- **Early Exits:** When a condition is satisfied, use early return statements in functions to prevent needless processing.

- **Efficient Loop Management:** Break out of loops

once the intended outcome is achieved to prevent needless iterations.

- **Decrease I/O Operations:** Network and disk I/O consume a lot of energy. Reduce batch operations and data transfers as much as you can.

Early Exit Example:

```
def find_value(arr, target):
    for value in arr:
        if value == target:
            return True
    return False
```

Making Use of Energy Profiling Instruments While Developing

Developers can determine which areas of their code use the most energy by using energy profiling tools. Through the integration of these technologies into the development process, teams may maximize energy efficiency by making data-driven decisions.

Popular Tools for Energy Profiling:

- **Intel Power Gadget:** Tracks Intel CPU power usage in real time.
- **GreenLab:** Offers energy measurements for various program components.
- **PyJoules:** An application and script energy consumption profiling Python library.

The Best Ways to Use Profiling Tools:

- Energy profiling should be incorporated into the development lifecycle, particularly during the testing and debugging stages.
- **Benchmarking:** To gauge improvements, compare energy consumption before and after code optimizations.
- **Automated Alerts:** Establish acceptable energy consumption criteria and get notifications when the code goes over them.

7.2 Methods of Software Optimization

Beyond coding conventions, software optimization strategies can instantly improve energy efficiency by dynamically modifying how apps communicate with hardware. Task scheduling, dynamic voltage and frequency scaling (DVFS), adaptive workloads, and energy-efficient operating systems are all covered in this area.

Task Scheduling with Adaptive Workloads

Adaptive workloads make sure that resources are used effectively by redistributing computational activities according to current conditions. This method works particularly well for cloud-based and multi-threaded apps.

Adaptive Workload Strategies:

- Distribute work equally among processors to prevent overtaxing some cores while leaving others idle. This is known as load balancing.
- **Idle Time Reduction:** Plan your work to cut down on CPU and GPU idle time. Hardware can more efficiently enter low-power modes by grouping activities together.

- **Setting priorities:** Defer non-essential tasks until times when demand is low and give energy-efficient chores a higher priority.

The algorithms used for task scheduling are:

- The round robin method divides work equally, although it might need to be modified for energy efficiency.
- **Greedy Scheduling:** To reduce overall power consumption, jobs that can be finished promptly are prioritized.
- **Energy-Aware Scheduling:** Takes energy consumption data into account when assigning tasks.

Dynamic Frequency and Voltage Scaling (DVFS)

DVFS is a technology that dynamically modifies a processor's voltage and clock frequency in response to workload needs. This makes it possible for processors to run at lower power levels when activity is lower.

DVFS Operation:

- **High-Performance Mode:** The processor runs at higher frequencies to optimize performance when the workload is severe.
- **Low-Power Mode:** The processor lowers voltage and frequency to conserve energy when it is idle or not in use.

Implementation Techniques:

- **Operating System Support:** DVFS is supported by power management settings in contemporary operating systems such as Windows and Linux.
- **Application-Level Control**: For more precise power management, developers can integrate DVFS controls into apps.

Energy-Saving Platforms and Operating Systems

Because operating systems (OS) control the distribution and use of hardware resources, they have a big impact on energy efficiency.

The Energy-Efficient OS's features include:

- **Power Management Policies:** Power profiles (e.g., Balanced, Power Saver, High Performance) are available on modern OS platforms and modify resource allocation according to user requirements.

- **Idle State Management:** Operating systems such as Windows (with Sleep States and Connected Standby) and Linux (with TLP or Powertop) optimize idle periods to reduce energy consumption.

- **Resource Virtualization:** To conserve energy, virtual machines and containers can be paused or shut down when not in use.

7.3 Methodologies for Green Software Development

Long-term energy efficiency and environmental responsibility are encouraged when sustainability principles are incorporated into the software development lifecycle (SDLC). How developers, sustainability specialists, and the larger IT community may work together to include green practices into software projects is covered in this section.

Integrating Sustainability into the Lifecycle of Software

Stages of the Sustainable SDLC:

1. One of the main requirements in project specifications should be energy efficiency, according to the requirements analysis.

- Take into account how software features affect the environment and give priority to those that use the fewest resources.

2. Design Phase:

- Create energy-efficient architectures, like microservices for scalability and event-driven models.
- Improve data flows to cut down on pointless processing.

3. Development and Coding:

- Use profiling tools and adhere to energy-efficient coding techniques.
- Keep track of the code's energy-saving strategies for

future usage.

4. Testing and Deployment:

- Include functional and performance testing in addition to energy efficiency testing.
- Reduce unnecessary builds and deployments by streamlining deployment workflows.

5. Maintenance and Updates:

- Constantly check software for energy efficiency and make necessary adjustments.
- Inefficient legacy code should be retired or redesigned.

Cooperation Between Sustainability Specialists and Developers

Collaboration between technical and environmental experts is beneficial for software development that is sustainable.

Optimal Methods for Cooperation:

- Incorporate sustainability specialists into

development teams to offer perspectives on mitigating environmental impact.

- **Continuous Evaluations:** Review energy efficiency during sprint retrospectives and code audits.
- **Training and Education:** Educate developers on energy-efficient design concepts and green coding techniques.

Promoting Green Practice Adoption in the IT Sector

For a broad impact, encouraging green practices throughout the sector is crucial.

Inspirational Techniques:

- **Open Source Initiatives:** Distribute tools and code libraries that use less energy.
- **Industry Guidelines:** Encourage groups that provide standards and guidelines for sustainable software, such as the Green Software Foundation.
- **Knowledge Sharing:** To promote and discuss energy-efficient development approaches, hold conferences, workshops, and webinars.

Since software controls how hardware resources are used, it is essential to energy efficiency. Developers can drastically lower energy consumption by implementing green methodology into the software lifecycle, utilizing software optimization techniques, and implementing energy-efficient coding practices. Sustainable software improves performance, lowers expenses, and fosters long-term technical resilience in addition to helping the environment.

CHAPTER 8

Integrating Renewable Energy into IT

The environmental impact of the IT industry's activities is growing in importance as it continues to grow. Switching IT infrastructure to renewable energy sources has become a crucial tactic as the urgency of addressing climate change increases. Incorporating renewable energy into IT not only lowers carbon emissions but also advances sustainability objectives, improves a company's brand, and may result in long-term financial savings. This chapter examines the ways in which IT infrastructure might switch to renewable energy sources, the function of energy storage in preserving dependability, and the significance of tracking and disclosing renewable energy use to promote accountability and transparency.

8.1 Making the Switch to Renewable IT Infrastructure

Advantages and Difficulties of Adoption of Renewable

Energy

Renewable Energy's Advantages for IT Infrastructure

1. Decreased Carbon Footprint: IT organizations can significantly lower greenhouse gas emissions related to their operations by utilizing solar, wind, hydro, or geothermal energy.

2. Energy Cost Stability: By reducing dependency on fossil fuels, renewable energy protects businesses from geopolitical risks and volatile energy prices.

3. Regulatory Compliance: Stricter environmental laws are being introduced in numerous nations and areas. Businesses can maintain compliance with these changing regulations by using renewable energy.

4. Enhanced Corporate Image: Using renewable energy shows a dedication to sustainability, which improves brand recognition and attracts investors and customers who care about the environment.

5. Long-Term Cost Savings: Renewable energy sources like solar and wind provide lower operating costs over time, despite potentially significant initial investments.

Adoption of Renewable Energy Faces Difficulties:

1. Intermittency: Depending on the weather and time of day, solar and wind power can fluctuate. Strong backup and storage solutions are necessary because of this unpredictability.

2. High Initial Costs: Making the switch to renewable energy frequently necessitates large upfront expenditures for infrastructure, such as geothermal, wind, or solar panels.

3. Infrastructure Compatibility: To successfully integrate renewable energy sources, legacy IT systems may require major changes.

4. Geographical Limitations: Not all renewable energy sources are appropriate for every region. For instance, places with less sunlight make solar energy less feasible.

Case Studies on Pioneering IT Companies

1. Google: Google has led the way in the use of renewable energy. Google's offices and data centers were powered entirely by renewable energy by 2017. The business invests in renewable energy projects across the globe and uses a combination of solar and wind power. Google secures energy at steady rates and contributes to the financing of renewable infrastructure through Power Purchase Agreements (PPAs).

2. Microsoft: By 2030, Microsoft aims to be carbon negative. To power its data centers, the corporation combines hydro, wind, and solar energy. To maximize utilization, Microsoft also makes investments in cutting-edge energy storage and AI-powered energy management systems.

3. Amazon Web Services (AWS): By 2025, AWS plans to run all of its infrastructure worldwide entirely on renewable energy. In addition to creating energy-efficient data centers, the corporation has started large-scale wind and solar projects.

Techniques to Guarantee Scalability and Reliability

Strategies that strike a balance between operational reliability and sustainability are necessary when switching IT infrastructure to renewable energy.

1. Hybrid Energy Models: To reduce intermittency, combine conventional energy with renewable sources.

- Data centers that run on solar energy during the day and transition to grid or battery power at night are one example.

2. Geographic Diversification: To ensure constant energy supply, disperse data centers among places with varying renewable strengths (for example, solar electricity in sunny regions and wind power along the coast).

3. Microgrids:

- Install regional renewable energy networks that are resilient and dependable and can function apart from the main grid.

4. Demand Response Systems:

- Modify IT tasks according to energy supply. Run non-essential operations, for instance, when renewable energy production is at its peak.

8.2 Solutions for Energy Storage and Backup

Advanced Storage and Batteries' Contribution to IT Sustainability

Energy storage devices are essential for maintaining a steady supply of electricity, especially when depending on sporadic renewable energy sources like wind and solar. Advanced storage technologies, such as batteries, aid in bridging the gap between energy production and consumption.

How Energy Storage Works in IT:

- **Backup electricity:** Offers instant electricity in the event of an outage or when renewable energy production is low.

- The process of load shifting involves storing excess renewable energy during periods of high generation and releasing it during periods of high demand.
- **Grid Stability:** Balances variations in supply and demand to help stabilize the electrical grid.

Cutting Edge Storage Technologies: Beyond Solid-State

1. The most popular storage option for IT infrastructure is Lithium-Ion Batteries.

- **Advantages:** Reliability, quick charging, and high energy density.
- **Cons:** Short lifespan and environmental issues associated with lithium mining.

2. In contrast to lithium-ion batteries, solid-state batteries are a new technology that offer a higher energy density and a longer lifespan.

- Benefits include increased efficiency and a lower chance of overheating.
- Problems with scalability and high manufacturing costs are obstacles.

3. Flow Batteries: These batteries are perfect for large-scale applications since they store energy using liquid electrolytes.

- Long cycle life and scalability are advantages.
- Use Case: Data centers that need a lot of energy storage.

4. Hydrogen Fuel Cells:

- Use a chemical reaction to transform stored hydrogen into electrical power.
- Benefits include long-term storage potential, excellent efficiency, and zero emissions.
- **Obstacles:** The infrastructure needed to produce and distribute hydrogen is still being developed.

Hybrid Methods for Optimal Performance

Reliability and efficiency can be increased by combining various energy storage methods.

Hybrid System Examples:

- **Battery + Hydrogen Backup:** For lengthy backup

during protracted outages, use hydrogen fuel cells and lithium-ion batteries for short-term electricity.

- **Renewable Energy + Flywheel Storage**: Batteries manage long-term storage, while flywheels supply short-term energy bursts.

8.3 Tracking and Documenting the Use of Renewable Energy

Resources for Monitoring the Integration of Renewable Energy

Transparency and the management of sustainability goals depend on accurate reporting and monitoring of renewable energy use. Organizations can monitor their energy use and integration of renewable energy sources with the use of a variety of technologies and platforms.

Important Platforms and Tools:

1. Energy Management Systems (EMS):
- Offer real-time energy consumption and source monitoring.

- Examples include the Desigo CC from Siemens and the EcoStruxure from Schneider Electric.

2. Software for Tracking Renewable Energy:

- Monitors the production and acquisition of renewable energy.
- Examples include the Energy Star Portfolio Manager and the Microsoft Sustainability Calculator.

3. Smart Meters and IoT Sensors:

- Gather detailed information on energy generation and consumption at various locations inside the IT infrastructure.

Certification and Adherence to International Guidelines

A company's dedication to sustainability and renewable energy is demonstrated by its certifications.

Relevant Certifications and Standards:

- **RE100:** An international program for businesses

dedicated to using only renewable energy.

- **ISO 50001:** An energy management standard that aids businesses in enhancing their energy efficiency.

- **Green-e Certification:** Verifies that renewable energy credits (RECs) adhere to consumer protection and environmental regulations.

Highlighting Stakeholder Engagement Accomplishments

Building confidence with stakeholders, such as consumers, investors, and staff, can be achieved by open reporting and showcasing renewable energy accomplishments.

Effective Communication Techniques:

1. Sustainability Reports:

- Every year, publish sustainability reports that include information on goals, accomplishments, and the use of renewable energy.

2. Highlighting successful renewable energy projects and their effects on operations is the second goal of the Press

Releases and Case Studies.

3. Involve on Social Media:

- Disseminate updates and achievements to raise awareness and motivate colleagues in the sector.

4. Third-Party Audits: Verify the veracity of renewable energy claims via impartial audits.

A crucial first step in accomplishing sustainability objectives is incorporating renewable energy into IT infrastructure. IT companies may drastically lessen their environmental effect by switching to renewable energy, putting innovative storage technologies in place, and closely monitoring energy consumption. This shift improves operational resilience, cost effectiveness, and company reputation in addition to promoting global climate action. Although adopting renewable energy in IT is a difficult process, it is necessary for a sustainable digital future.

CHAPTER 9

FRAMEWORKS FOR POLICIES AND REGULATIONS

Governments and international organizations are creating laws and regulations to make sure that IT and other businesses embrace sustainable practices as the globe struggles with resource shortages, climate change, and rising energy demands. In order to shape energy-efficient operations, IT businesses must navigate a complicated web of regional, international, and industry-specific rules. This chapter examines important international laws, rewards for environmentally friendly behavior, and ways to stay in compliance with a changing regulatory environment.

9.1 International IT Energy Consumption Regulations

Summary of Important Frameworks and Policies

The goal of international laws and rules is to lower carbon emissions and promote energy efficiency in all aspects of

IT operations. In order to foster accountability, promote innovation, and guarantee that IT infrastructure is planned with sustainability in mind, these frameworks are essential.

1. The Paris Agreement: This historic worldwide agreement, which was ratified in 2015, commits signatories to keeping global warming far below 2°C, with efforts to keep it at 1.5°C. The need for IT companies to connect their operations with national promises to minimize greenhouse gas (GHG) emissions which include switching to renewable energy sources and adopting energy-efficient practices is growing.

2. The European Green Deal: The EU's aim to become climate neutral by 2050 is outlined in the European Green Deal, which was introduced in 2019. It introduces regulations such as the Corporate Sustainability Reporting Directive (CSRD) and the Energy Efficiency Directive (EED), which require big businesses to reveal their carbon footprint and energy consumption. It is anticipated that data centers, which use a lot of energy, will meet stricter efficiency requirements and cut emissions.

3. The Energy Policy Act of the United States (EPAct):

Guidelines and incentives for energy efficiency in IT and other industries are provided under this policy. Organizations must record their energy use, and federal data centers must achieve certain efficiency goals. The statute promotes the use of renewable energy sources and devices with Energy Star certification.

China's dual carbon goals are to reach carbon neutrality by 2060 and peak carbon emissions by 2030. These objectives must guide the strategy of IT businesses doing business in China, with an emphasis on energy conservation and the adoption of green technologies.

Regulation Variations by Region

Global objectives lay the groundwork, but regional rules differ greatly, reflecting local economic situations, resources, and priorities.

Europe:

- **Strict Regulations:** The EU enforces strict laws, including environmental requirements and the

General Data Protection Regulation (GDPR). Businesses are required to reveal sustainability information and adhere to energy efficiency regulations.

- **Energy Efficiency Targets**: Data centers must embrace renewable energy sources and achieve Power Usage Effectiveness (PUE) standards.

North America:

- **Federal and State-Level Policies:** The United States has federal laws, but several states (like California) have extra rules aimed at reducing emissions and improving energy efficiency.
- **Incentives Over Mandates:** Policies frequently use grants and tax breaks as incentives to promote voluntary compliance.

Asia-Pacific:

- **Different Policies, Rapid Growth**: China, South Korea, Japan, and other nations have set high goals to become carbon neutral. Regulations differ greatly, though, with some areas prioritizing the reduction of coal use while others make significant investments in renewable energy.

How International Agreements Affect IT Procedures

A comprehensive framework for environmental responsibility is established by international agreements like the Paris Agreement and the Sustainable Development Goals (SDGs) of the United Nations. These contracts have an impact on IT procedures by:

- Establishing Emission Reduction Objectives: Businesses must cut carbon emissions in accordance with their respective countries' contributions to international objectives.
- **Encouraging Transparency:** Companies are required to disclose their energy usage and sustainability initiatives.
- **Inspiring Innovation:** IT firms are encouraged to embrace cutting-edge energy-efficient technologies and renewable energy solutions by conforming to international standards.

In addition to reducing the risk of fines, adherence to these international accords improves stakeholder trust and company reputation.

9.2 Rewards for Eco-Friendly Activities

Grants and Tax Benefits for Using Green IT

To encourage IT companies to embrace sustainable practices, governments around the world provide financial incentives. The cost of switching to renewable energy and energy-efficient operations is lessened by these incentives.

1. Tax Credits:

- **Renewable Energy Tax Credits:** Investing in renewable energy infrastructure, including solar panels or wind turbines for data centers, can result in tax credits in many nations.
- Businesses that update to servers, cooling systems, and storage devices certified by Energy Star are eligible for tax deductions under the Energy-Efficient Equipment Credits.

2. Grants and Subsidies:

- Research and development of energy-efficient technologies can be funded through the Green Innovation Grants.

- **Sustainability Transition Funds:** These funds help businesses upgrade their outdated systems to satisfy energy efficiency requirements.

The Investment Tax Credit (ITC) in the United States offers a 30% credit for investments in renewable energy. Horizon Europe funding is available from the European Commission for projects involving sustainable digital transformation.

Partnerships and Initiatives Led by the Industry

The IT sector itself encourages sustainability through cooperative projects and alliances in addition to government incentives.

- An industry group called Green Grid is dedicated to enhancing data center effectiveness and encouraging environmentally friendly IT procedures.

- **Data Center Pact for Climate Neutrality:** By

2030, more than 25 European cloud and data center companies have committed to becoming climate neutral.

- **Tech Giants' Alliances**: Businesses such as Google, Microsoft, and Amazon collaborate on projects to create renewable energy sources and energy-efficient data centers.

Working Together with Governments to Promote Policies

IT companies may influence rules and make sure they are realistic and attainable by interacting with legislators.

- **Public-Private Dialogues:** Gatherings where government representatives and business executives work together to create well-rounded policies.
- **Policy Recommendations:** IT companies can offer frameworks for accomplishing sustainability objectives and insights into the viability of suggested rules.
- **Pilot Programs:** Collaborating with governments to evaluate energy-efficient techniques or new

technology in practical settings.

These partnerships ensure that excessively stringent laws do not impede industry growth while also assisting in the development of successful policies.

9.3 Handling Compliance Issues

Keeping abreast with changing regulations

In order to stay compliant, IT firms need to stay educated about the constantly changing regulatory landscape.

Methods for Keeping Up to Date:
- **Regulatory Monitoring Services:** Websites such as LexisNexis or Compliance.ai offer up-to-date information on regulatory modifications.
- Joining organizations such as the International Association of IT Asset Managers (IAITAM) gives access to best practices and regulatory knowledge.
- **Legal and Compliance Teams:** Committed groups or consultants make sure businesses correctly understand and apply legislation.

Audits and Certifications for Sustainable Practices

Regular audits and certifications reflect an organization's commitment to compliance and sustainability.

- **ISO 14001:** Environmental management certification for companies dedicated to minimizing their environmental impact is one of the key audits and certifications.
- **Leadership in Energy and Environmental Design, or LEED:** Accreditation for data centers and other sustainable construction principles.
- High-performance and low-impact data centers are identified by the Building Research Establishment Environmental Assessment Method, or BREEAM.

The following are some advantages of audits:
- Identify Gaps: Point out areas where compliance and energy efficiency need to be improved.
- **Build Credibility:** Stakeholder confidence is increased by third-party validation.
- **Ongoing Enhancement:** Audits offer practical

information for sustained viability.

Reducing Non-Compliance Risks

Regulation violations may result in fines, harm to one's reputation, and interruptions to business operations.

Strategies for Mitigating Risk:

1. **Continuous Training**: Inform staff members on best practices and compliance needs.
2. **Compliance Audits:** To find and fix compliance problems, conduct recurring internal and external audits.
3. **Sturdy Documentation:** Keep thorough records of your energy use, sustainability initiatives, and compliance tasks.
4. **Incident Response Plans:** Create procedures to deal with possible infractions of compliance in a timely and open manner.

IT firms that are dedicated to sustainability must successfully navigate the complicated world of policy and regulatory frameworks. IT leaders may promote energy-efficient practices and help achieve global climate goals by being aware of international rules, utilizing financial incentives, and implementing strong compliance measures. Active interaction with legislators and business partners guarantees that rules are workable and efficient, promoting a sustainable digital future.

CHAPTER 10

ENERGY-EFFICIENT COMPUTING'S FUTURE

Energy-efficient computing has evolved from a side issue to a fundamental tenet of IT operations across the globe. The IT sector must embrace cutting-edge technologies, strategic planning, and revolutionary business processes in order to adapt to the growing energy demands and more noticeable effects of climate change. The future trends influencing IT energy efficiency are examined in this chapter, along with how businesses should get ready for the changes anticipated in the late 2020s and the wider societal effects of these developments.

10.1 Trends Influencing IT Energy Efficiency

AI Developments in Energy Management

The use of artificial intelligence (AI) in IT infrastructure is revolutionizing energy efficiency. AI can optimize energy use in previously unachievable ways through intelligent decision-making and real-time data analysis.

Primary AI Uses in Energy Management:

1. **Dynamic Resource Allocation:** AI systems assess server loads and real-time reassign work to reduce energy usage. AI has the potential to decrease power consumption by reducing the number of active servers through the identification of unused resources and the consolidation of workloads.

2. **Predictive Maintenance:** IT managers can take proactive measures to fix problems by using AI to anticipate possible equipment breakdowns or inefficiencies before they happen. By doing this, downtime is decreased and energy waste from broken equipment is prevented.

3. **Smart Cooling Systems:** AI-powered cooling systems may dynamically modify airflow and temperature in data centers by using real-time heat maps. This lessens the energy load connected with conventional cooling techniques by guaranteeing that cooling is directed just where it is required.

4. **Energy Forecasting:** AI can forecast future energy

requirements by analyzing previous data, which makes energy purchase and usage planning more precise and effective.

Advances in Edge and Decentralized Computing

Decentralized and edge computing are becoming essential solutions for energy-efficient IT operations as the amount of data produced by IoT devices, sensors, and smart systems keeps increasing.

The following are some advantages of edge computing for energy efficiency:

1. **Decreased Data Transfer Needs:** Edge computing eliminates the need to send massive amounts of data to centralized data centers by processing data closer to the source. As a result, data transmission energy costs are reduced.

2. **Localized Processing:** By executing processing activities in real-time, edge devices can minimize latency and the requirement for constant cloud communication. This saves electricity in addition to enhancing performance.

3. **Optimized Infrastructure:** By enabling enterprises to place energy-efficient, lightweight infrastructure near end users, edge computing lessens the strain on central data centers.

Decentralized Networks: By removing the need for centralized servers, more efficiently allocating workloads, and improving security without requiring a large amount of computing, blockchain and distributed ledger technologies are also helping to reduce energy consumption.

Increased Attention on Net-Zero IT Operations

For many IT companies, reaching net-zero carbon emissions has become a top priority. In addition to cutting energy use, the drive toward net-zero operations also entails investing in sustainable practices and offsetting any emissions that remain.

Net-Zero IT Strategies:

1. **100% Renewable Energy:** Converting IT infrastructure and data centers to renewable energy sources like hydroelectric, solar, and wind.

2. **Carbon Offsetting:** Funding initiatives like carbon capture technologies or reforestation that take carbon out of the atmosphere.

3. **Circular Economy Practices**: Using the reduce, reuse, and recycle principles to prolong the life cycle of hardware and reduce electronic waste.

4. **Transparency and Reporting:** Providing stakeholders and the general public with regular updates on energy consumption, carbon emissions, and sustainability measures.

By pledging to attain net-zero operations by 2030, corporations like Google, Microsoft, and Amazon Web Services have set industry standards.

10.2 Getting Ready for the Late 2020s Transition

Early Adoption of Emerging Technologies

Significant developments in energy-efficient computing technologies are anticipated in the late 2020s. To stay competitive and sustainable, forward-thinking companies should get ready by implementing these advances as soon as possible.

Key Emerging Technologies:

1. **Quantum Computing:** This technology is still in its infancy, but it has the potential to solve complicated issues using a lot less energy than traditional computers.

2. **Photonic Computing:** Data transmission via light rather than electricity can significantly lower heat production and energy consumption.

3. **Neuromorphic Computing:** Designed to outperform conventional CPUs and GPUs in computations, neuromorphic processors are modeled after the human brain.

4. **Advanced Cooling Solutions:** More effective methods of controlling heat in data centers are provided by technologies such as liquid nitrogen-based cooling systems and immersion cooling.

Expanding Solutions to Have a Broad Effect

Energy-efficient techniques need to be scalable across

international IT infrastructure in order to make a significant difference.

Scaling Techniques:

1. The establishment of industry-wide energy efficiency standards guarantees that techniques can be duplicated across various businesses and geographical areas.

2. **Collaborative Innovation:** Creating scalable energy-efficient solutions by collaborating with other businesses, academic institutions, and governmental entities.

3. The implementation of successful pilot projects on a broader scale, known as "global rollouts," guarantees that energy-efficient techniques are not restricted to a particular department or location.

Strategic Research and Development Investments for Sustainability

Research and development (R&D) spending is essential to propelling the upcoming generation of energy-efficient computer advancements.

R&D Focus Areas:

1. **Material Science:** creating novel materials that boost processor, storage, and semiconductor efficiency.

2. **AI and Automation:** Improving AI algorithms to automate sustainable procedures and better optimize energy use.

3. **Energy Storage:** To facilitate the integration of renewable energy, battery and energy storage technologies are being advanced.

4. The study of how digital technologies and physical infrastructure may cooperate to increase energy efficiency is known as Cyber-Physical Systems.

Businesses who put sustainability research and development first will not only lessen their environmental effect but also obtain a competitive advantage in a market that is becoming more and more influenced by eco-conscious laws and consumers.

10.3 Extended Effects on Society and IT

Making IT a Leader in Sustainability

The IT sector is in a unique position to spearhead the global sustainability movement. IT can serve as a potent model for energy-efficient practices because of its creative culture, extensive resources, and sway over all industries.

Prospective IT Leadership Positions:

1. **Setting Industry Standards:** creating and advancing sustainable and energy-efficient best practices.
2. Working together with governments to develop policies that promote sustainable innovation is known as public-private partnerships.
3. **Accountability and Transparency:** Setting the standard for accountability and transparent reporting about environmental effects.

Using IT to Support Global Green Initiatives

IT is essential to facilitating and supporting sustainability initiatives in a variety of sectors.

Examples of Green Initiatives Driven by IT:

1. Using IT to build intelligent energy distribution networks that maximize electricity use is known as "smart grids."

2. **Sustainable Agriculture:** Using AI and IoT sensors to optimize water use, minimize chemical inputs, and monitor soil health.

3. **Green Transportation:** Assisting with smart traffic management systems, autonomous driving, and electric car infrastructure.

IT contributes to the global advancement of sustainability by serving as the technology foundation for these programs.

Motivating Inter-Sector Cooperation for Energy Efficiency

Collaboration across industry is necessary to achieve a sustainable future. Energy efficiency-focused cross-industry collaborations can be sparked by the IT sector.

Cross-Industry Collaboration Strategies:

1. **Knowledge Sharing:** Organizing seminars, conferences, and forums where sectors can exchange ideas and best practices.

2. **Collaborative Research Projects:** Working together on research projects to create innovative technologies that use less energy.

3. **Supply Chain Partnerships:** Assisting partners and suppliers in integrating sustainable practices across the supply chain.

AI developments, decentralized system advancements, and a strong dedication to net-zero operations are shaping the future of energy-efficient computing. IT companies must scale successful solutions, invest strategically in R&D, and embrace emerging technologies early in order to be ready for the changes of the late 2020s. By adopting this, the IT industry may become a pioneer in sustainability, facilitating international green projects and encouraging cooperation across industries. In addition to lessening the impact on the environment, this team effort will spur innovation and guarantee a more sustainable future for everybody.

ABOUT THE AUTHOR

 Author and thought leader in the IT field Taylor Royce is well known. He has a two-decade career and is an expert at tech trend analysis and forecasting, which enables a wide audience to understand complicated concepts.

Royce's considerable involvement in the IT industry stemmed from his passion with technology, which he developed during his computer science studies. He has extensive knowledge of the industry because of his experience in both software development and strategic consulting.

Known for his research and lucidity, he has written multiple best-selling books and contributed to esteemed tech periodicals. Translations of Royce's books throughout the world demonstrate his impact.

Royce is a well-known authority on emerging technologies and their effects on society, frequently requested as a speaker at international conferences and as a guest on tech podcasts. He promotes the development of ethical technology, emphasizing problems like data privacy and the digital divide.

In addition, with a focus on sustainable industry growth, Royce mentors upcoming tech experts and supports IT education projects. Taylor Royce is well known for his ability to combine analytical thinking with technical know-how. He sees a time when technology will ethically benefit humanity.

www.ingramcontent.com/pod-product-compliance
Lightning Source LLC
Chambersburg PA
CBHW071003050326
40689CB00014B/3466